The Complete You Architecture

Learn How to Rise Above and Standout in Your Career

Dr. Chris Bradshaw

This book has two dedications.

To my family.

Who have supported me through the highs and lows of the rollercoaster I call a career, the personal pursuit of a doctorate, and my journey in writing this book. You are my purpose.

And, to you.

The motivated, constant learner who is often overlooked or hasn't broken through to your true potential. We share this path.

Contents

Introduction

"I always liked those moments of epiphany when you have the next destination."

- Academy Award Winner Brad Pitt

My moment of epiphany came several years ago while working as a strategy consultant with one of the world's largest consulting firms. I witnessed a moment of leadership greatness that transformed my view of personal and career development.

I was in my fourth year as a strategy consultant at one of the world's largest consulting companies. As part of my job, I partnered with companies that needed to reinvent their go-to-market strategies, product and channel offerings, or enter/exit markets. They were usually well-established companies that were bleeding revenue and seeing their profit margins erode due to competitive pressures, shifting market conditions, or poor management. I described my work as "restarting stalled or failing businesses."

And in July 2014, I had one of my most demanding clients. I led a multi-day offsite executive retreat in Colorado with a high-profile, blue-chip company.

The client, a household name who has been in business for a century, was in a desperate spot. A decade earlier, a new competitor (for now, we will call Company A) had entered the market with a fresh, innovative product ahead of the curve.

The early years for Company A were tough, and this caused many of the established industry giants to ignore it. As with most emerging technologies and companies, this new competitor struggled with production, consumer acceptance, and market reach. Thus, its revenue growth was slow, underperforming Wall Street expectations.

But this was 2014, and this young competitor had just found its stride. Their newly found momentum started to create a lot of panic within the executive offices of my client. Revenue at this small competitor had jumped from $413 million in 2012 to $2 billion in 2013, and they would go on to close 2014 with $3.2 billion in sales. That's enormous growth!

To make things worse, my client's executives had known about this emerging threat for years because their market research had shown that consumer trends were shifting, and the company was not evolving to meet them. From my point of view, the executive team's arrogance had failed the company, its tens of thousands of employees, and its stockholders. In an example of their superiority, in 2012, the CEO publicly said that this small competitor was "a fad that wouldn't affect our domestic business."

Fast forward to the present. Tesla reported revenue of $53.8 billion in 2021 and is the most valuable automotive company globally (by a lot!).

Not bad business for a fad.

So, now that you know a little bit of the context, let me tell you about the moment I became consumed with studying soft skills.

The goal of the offsite executive meeting in Colorado that July was to refresh the client's product and marketing strategy. This retreat included a mix of junior and senior executives from the client who was among the best and brightest in the company and even the industry.

However, this wasn't what you might think an executive retreat with 30-plus white-collar leaders would be like. There was no golf, hiking, or fishing, and since it was summer, there was no skiing. Spouses, partners, and families were not invited. Instead, it was 12-hour days followed by team dinners and drinks at the resort bar that were just places to continue the discussions from earlier in the day. There was absolute panic.

We spent the first two days moving between large room presentations and small breakout rooms with exercises focused on two essential topics. The first was how to quickly create a viable electric vehicle (EV) alternative to Tesla's Model S (introduced in 2012). The second was how to directly attack Tesla using the company's massive marketing platform and budget to pull consumers back to their existing products.

But, those topics would drastically change by mid-morning on the third day. What I didn't realize at that particular moment was how much my life would change simultaneously.

A group of product development engineers and designers had just presented a product roadmap to the entire group. It outlined the budget and resources needed to quickly bring a new EV through concept, proto-type, testing, and then to production. The room broke out in chaos.

Everyone from the company's CEO to the most junior person in the room started showering the presenters with cheers, a few simple questions, and statements of support. I couldn't help but think this was a good thing.

As the facilitator, I tried but could not reel everyone back into a single discussion. The entire room was on their feet, consumed with side conversations where everyone tried to talk over each other using a progressively louder voice. Excitement and a giant sigh of relief were spreading.

I was in the back of the room and started to move to the front so I could better bring order to the room and move us on to the next item on the agenda. That's when I noticed her. Dressed in a smart casual blue blouse and long dark skirt, she was in the middle row, about five seats in from the side where I was walking up from the back of the room. She was the only person in the room still sitting and, I am pretty sure, the only person not talking. She was a Vice President in the Human Resources depart-ment, and I recall her being a good participant who was willing to share her thoughts during the first two days. So, yeah. It was odd that she was still sitting, not saying anything. But then it happened.

She stood up and looked at one of the designers who had just finished presenting. Using a measured voice, she calmly said, "This is a brilliant approach to product development, and it's why we have been so successful over the decades." A few people close to her turned to listen. One individual was even quick to agree by adding, "I know, this is so exciting."

I stopped just feet away and watched what happened next.

Her following words altered the direction of our remaining time at the retreat and changed the future direction of the entire company. With a few more of her executive peers looking toward her, she continued, "But while it's great, it is also why we are in this situation and at this retreat. I fear we can't win against Tesla with the same thinking and approach that put us in this room."

A few more executives on our side of the room turned to her, including the client's most senior product developer. This individual needed no introduction during the presentation, which had just concluded. He was a giant in the industry. The company's Chief Marketing Officer (CMO) later described him as the sole reason two flagship vehicles existed. And that his contribution to the company could be measured "in billions of dollars."

The astonished look on his face made it evident that he was not in agreement and the sting behind his tone when he replied to her made it even more apparent that he found her comments insulting. His words, style, and slightly elevated voice pulled the entire room into this one conversation. This HR VP, a junior executive, probably in her early to mid-40s, was now in the crosshairs of one of the industry's most respected car designers. And he let her know it.

"I don't think you fully understand my team's work and how important it is for us to remain focused on what we do best," were his exact words back to her.

All eyes, including the CEO's and several of the c-suite team members, were locked on her. As a consultant who had seen this type of power stare down before working with other companies, I was sure she would retreat to the safety found in agreeing with the lead product developer. But she didn't. She took over the conversation and won!

Looking directly at the lead developer, she nodded in agreement and then expanded on her point of view. "I understand and have the deepest respect for what you and your team have done. You are the best in the industry. But, the industry has changed." She pointed to the PowerPoint slide left on the large projector screen. It showed a detailed version of the EV development timeline covering multiple years.

She stepped out of the row of chairs where she had been, walked right past me, the lead developer, and proceeded to the front of the room. She turned to face everyone. "If our goal is to take on Tesla and win, we must first change our mindset. It starts with recognizing that we can't do that with business as usual." She pointed to the screen and firmly stated, "Yes, this is brilliant. But, I don't see us winning this way."

Over the next few minutes, she masterfully dissected the EV plan by highlighting where Tesla had won with design, innovation, and consumers. She used data, not opinion, to point out where she felt the plan was flawed. She interacted with the team using elegance and rose to the moment.

In a few short moments, this junior HR VP had changed many of the minds in the room, destroyed my plan for the rest of the retreat, and set the wheels in motion for the company to rethink how they developed products.

While the executives discussed the implications of her suggestions and were formulating how to move forward over the next day and a half, I stood there partly confused and intrigued.

How did she do that?

How did her words break through to a room filled with some of the most influential executives in the automotive industry?

The questions I wanted to know were;

Why could I not do what she just did?

What was I lacking?

It was my moment of epiphany. I had to know why some leaders excelled and why most of us would fall short. But most importantly, I had to know what set her apart.

Hi. My name is Dr. Chris Bradshaw.

I am a researcher, an educator of soft skills, and the creator of Complete You Architecture™ (CYA). And the moment I just described to you is a true story that altered my professional career. As well as my life.

Here is why.

At that moment, standing in wonder at the side of the room, I had my next destination. I knew I needed to understand how this junior HR VP could steer a large group of opinionated, entrenched executives to agree that they needed to abandon decades of institutional knowledge to meet the challenges of a changing market. But that was the destination, not the motivation I would eventually need to get there.

I suspect you might already know quite a bit about the motivation to seek new knowledge to better yourself. It's the same burning drive behind you getting this book: we want more out of our careers and are not yet getting it.

We have a lot in common if you are nodding your head in agreement. I, too, have been where you might be now.

I have suffered from the frustration of not being recognized for my contribution at work.

I have experienced the self-doubt of not believing I was good enough to achieve my career goals.

I have seen peers advance faster and get paid more.

I have spent countless hours daydreaming about my next career step. The following job interview which would allow me to prove my worth to a hiring manager.

And my favorite daydream, that moment in time when I finally got what I thought I deserved!

You know what I mean. It's the title, the pay raise, the opportunity to show all those who passed on us that we deserved their admiration and to have had a chance to succeed. I wanted to rub their noses in it once I succeeded.

But, for me, the opposite has happened. I have hit a few bumps throughout my twenty-plus-year career in leadership and consulting. I have been laid off twice, fired once, and have had to reinvent myself professionally at least three times.

> *Funny fact about myself. I have been laid off and then fired by the same company. I was laid off during the 2008 economic crisis and later fired for cause after rejoining the company. Hence, my personal need for reinvention.*

Have you ever felt any of these same frustrations? Have you experienced similar setbacks in your career?

If so, you probably have tried to find ways to better yourself, as I have.

I turned to traditional education and returned to college for not one but two Master's degrees. I even went the professional certification route to gain what I thought was the experience hiring managers wanted to see.

The good news is that each time I reinvented myself, I found new success. At least for short periods.

The challenge I was facing might be the same one you are experiencing today. My career just never took off the way I thought it would. Instead, my career trajectory flattened, and I realized that I would not achieve what I felt I could.

Standing in a conference room in Colorado in July 2014, I had my moment of epiphany. Motivation meets epiphany.

Everything changed for me.

To understand how that Jr. VP altered the course of a major company and, in no short part, her career, I returned to college and earned a doctorate in leadership studies from the University of Southern California. Fight On, Trojans!

I devoted my studies, research, and personal time to peeling back the layers of contemporary literature to identify the true nuances of what sets individuals apart from their equally educated and talented peers. At the core of my work was to expose why some individuals achieve a higher career trajectory despite having the same education and on-the-job training as their peers.

What I discovered was that great leaders have elevated soft skills. And it is soft skills that have the most influence on your career development. But, truthfully, that is old news. For decades its been taught and well-documented in popular magazines and academic journals.

You will learn with the CYA that your success requires more than just having a single soft skill or a set of skills. You have to build a personal architecture of critical skills that are complementary and linked. Let me explain a little further.

Through my research, I found twelve soft skills are the most important to an individual's success. More importantly, employers are eager to find people who can demonstrate them. I discovered that these twelve skills could be categorized into three domains: how you think, feel, and act—much more on the three domains in Chapter 3.

Next, I found that those with a heightened level of maturity have learned how to link multiple skills together, as explained in Chapter 7.

I also discovered that popular topics such as leadership, decision-making, and strategic thinking are skill structures that must be developed using multiple soft skills that complement one another. See Chapter 8 for more on skill structures.

To boldly summarize the essence of what my research uncovered: As professionals with career and life ambitions, we have not been set up for success through traditional educational platforms or our employer's on-the-job training. We lack the practical knowledge of the soft skills crucial to our ability to stand out among peers and rise above our careers.

Thus, I created the Complete You Architecture™ based on my research and personal experiences. It is a research-driven approach to learning, strengthening, and linking the twelve soft skills proven to be the most critical to our career trajectory and success.

Image 1: The Complete You Architecture™

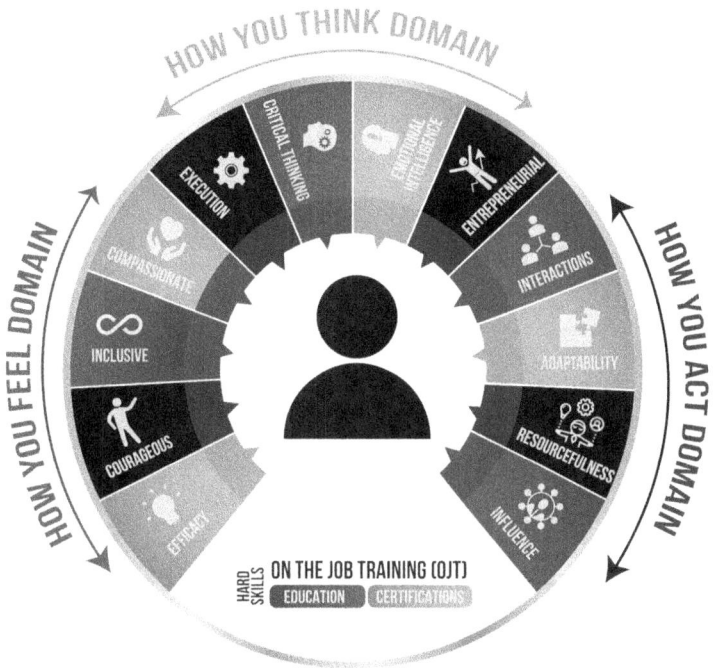

Many are the same soft skills I witnessed in 2014. Some of them are the classic ones you and I have conceptually learned before but perhaps never figured out how to apply in our careers. And last, a few of the skills are unique to the CYA.

So, now it's up to you.

Are you motivated? Are you ready to stand out and rise above your peers?

If so, let's get started.

How to Use This Workbook

For the best learning experience and to maximize your personal development, this workbook is divided into sections, chapters, and lessons.

A **section** is a complete body of work that comprises several chapters and subsequent lessons.

A **chapter** will focus on a single topic or skill and might include multiple lessons.

The **lessons** throughout this workbook are intended to provide you with the practical and applicable knowledge that you will need to start to master an existing or a new soft skill.

Knowledge without application is not going to help you reach your goals. This simplified learning approach will maximize your retention and help you achieve your learning goals faster:

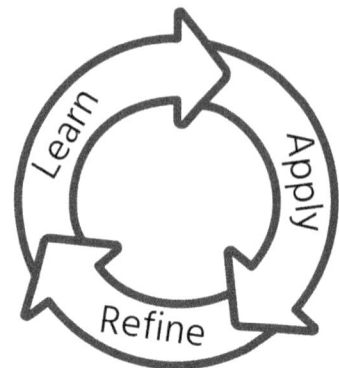

- To **Learn** is to consume new knowledge.
- To **Apply** is to use that knowledge as a new way of thinking or working.
- To **Refine** is to reflect on applying this new knowledge and making it fit into your personal situation.

Through your learning experience, we will often return to how you are applying and refining your skills. As you go through this workbook, be on the lookout for these special call-outs:

No Brainer Tips

These valuable tips are quick, straightforward ways you can start to rise above and stand out among your peers. They are called "no-brainers" because they require little effort.

Tough Talk

Like a punch on the chin, this "tough talk" is meant to catch your attention and provoke a reaction by telling you what you might already know but haven't yet come to grasp. Personal growth is achieved through being uncomfortable.

Warning

Be on the lookout for "warnings." These are more than just tips; they will help you along the way by avoiding common mistakes, missteps, and the occasional landmine that others have already learned the hard way.

Section 1 - Filling a Void

AT THE END of this section, you will:

- Understand the differences between two basic skill types and why the skills most critical to your success have not been well-taught.
- See the findings of a multi-year longitudinal research study.
- Be introduced to the Complete You Architecture™.
- Be able to differentiate the Complete You Architecture™ from other skill models.

Research Study Quick Facts (*As of May 2022)

- A longitudinal study that is > 4 years
- 73 International Organizations
- 1,238 Participants

Key Findings

- 4 out of 5 young professionals said their education did not prepare them with the soft skills needed to succeed once they entered the workforce.
- 41% of study participants (~507) self-identified as young professionals with less than five years in the workforce

- 87% of the participants agreed that soft skills were a development gap within their organizations.
- Two-thirds of participants reported their careers plateaued by the time they were 37 years old.

Research Study Demographics

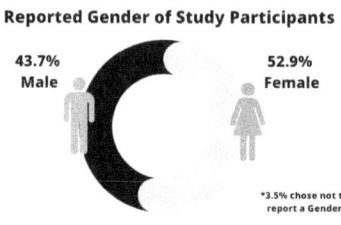

Reported Gender of Study Participants

43.7% Male

52.9% Female

*3.5% chose not to report a Gender

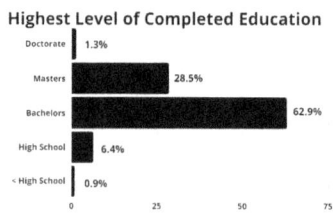

Highest Level of Completed Education

Doctorate	1.3%
Masters	28.5%
Bachelors	62.9%
High School	6.4%
< High School	0.9%

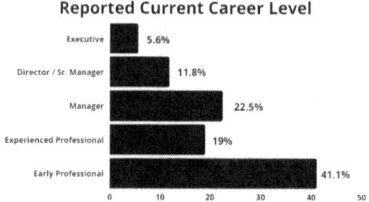

Reported Current Career Level

Executive	5.6%
Director / Sr. Manager	11.8%
Manager	22.5%
Experienced Professional	19%
Early Professional	41.1%

Chapter 1
Understanding the Different Skill Types

WE WORK in a society where skills determine our value. Your ability to perform a set of skills influences your paycheck, ability to provide for your family, career development, and many other tangible facets of life. While we can argue that specific skills are more valuable than others, we can not dispute their importance. For proof, look no further than the last time you applied for a job and prepared your resume or CV.

Even the interview process itself is an examination of your skills. The daunting task of turning your experience, education, strengths, and accomplishments into an eye-catching document that a recruiter or hiring manager will spend more than 5 seconds on is not a simple exercise. We then must endure an interview or two so a hiring manager can assess if our skills meet their hiring needs. The traditional job hiring process is a testament to how essential skills are to our success.

But are we focusing on the right ones? The research behind the CYA suggests that we do not. Allow me to explain.

Do you know that skills fall into two simple categories?

Do you understand their differences and why soft skills are more critical to your long-term career advancement? Yet most of our education and on-the-job training is focused on hard skills.

If you think that does not make much sense, you are right.

We are most accustomed to learning and exhibiting hard skills at work—commonly defined as technical or applicable knowledge that teaches you how to perform or complete a task.

For instance, a typical complex skill for a software developer would be coding. A nurse must know how to take a patient's vitals and administer medicines. A sales rep must understand how to demonstrate the product, features, and customer benefits of the items they sell.

Each of these is an example of the hard skills acquired through the factual, procedural, and conceptual knowledge (see Table 1) gained while earning a college degree, or more commonly, on-the-job training.

Table 1: Four Dimensions of Knowledge

Types of Knowledge in Revised Bloom's Taxonomy		Sub-Types
Factual Knowledge	Knowledge of	Terminology Specific Details and Elements
Conceptual Knowledge	knowledge of	Classifications and Categories Principles and Generalizations Theories, Models, and Structures
Procedural Knowledge	Knowledge of	Subject-specific Skills and Algorithms Subject-specific Techniques and Methods Criteria for Determining When to Use Appropriate Procedures
Meta-Cognitive Knowledge		Strategic Knowledge Knowledge about Cognitive Tasks Self-Knowledge

From Anderson, Lorin and David Krathwohl. A Taxonomy For Learning, Teaching and Assessing. New York: Longman, 2001.

Conversely, soft skills are personal traits, character attributes, or relational aptitudes. These are generally associated with metacognitive knowledge about oneself and how we think. Examples of soft skills would be how a nurse shows compassion to a patient in a lot of pain, how a manager can read a room while giving a presentation, and adjust her style to engage the audience better. Or how a junior executive can take control of a room to make a bold idea and have it accepted by her senior executives.

> *Tough Talk*
> *To plainly state the observed difference, hard skills get the required job done. In contrast, the right soft skills improve relationships, productivity, creativity, and career trajectory.*

This is why you see elevated soft skills in executives and senior managers. Individuals in those roles have moved past coding or demonstrating product, feature, and benefit descriptions to using skills associated with coaching, critical thinking, influencing others to act, etc.

That's not suggesting someone with a big fancy title has all the necessary soft skills to succeed. Having coached c-suite executives for over a decade, I can promise that even the highest-ranking leaders have blind spots and skill gaps.

Another critical difference between these two types is why hard skills are more widely taught during primary education or on-the-job training programs our employers provide and why soft skills are often not given as much attention. Measuring the new knowledge gained when learning a hard skill is extremely easy. Did the learner get the concept? Were they able to demonstrate it during training or on a test? Did they perform it when they returned to their job?

Organizations investing in hard skill training can easily correlate new knowledge and job performance to show a return on investment. In contrast, soft skills are much more challenging to measure and nearly impossible to associate with individual job improvement or organizational financial performance. The result is that too much time, money, and energy are spent on the least essential skills to your personal growth and development simply because they are easier to teach and measure.

My research proves that our ability to demonstrate an elevated maturity of soft skills will significantly impact our career trajectory more than hard skills.

Chapter 2
The Research and The Architecture

YEARS AGO, while studying for my doctorate, my research focused on working professionals' knowledge and motivational influences. Synthesizing across decades of academic and industry publications, I found a massive gap between the soft skills employers needed and those taught in colleges, professional certification courses, or on-the-job training programs.

As a research fellow, I extended my study to understand better the soft skills an individual needs to be successful. I found that 4 out of 5 young professionals say their education did not prepare them with the soft skills vital to their success in the workforce.

Determined to expand the awareness of this disparity and provide a data-driven solution, I began a multi-year research study that has gone on to include more than 1,200 participants from over 70 international organizations.

As of 2022, I am in my fourth year of this longitudinal study, and the findings show that there is a huge need for individuals to learn and master soft skills.

In addition to the results shared earlier, my research yielded the following results:

- Nearly three-quarters of the 73 organizations reported spending less than 25% of their overall training budgets on building employee soft skills. 87% of the study participants agreed that these skills were a development gap within their organizations.
- Two-thirds of the participants who classified themselves as middle managers claimed they had peaked in their careers by 37. This is what I refer to as career plateauing.
- During observations, individuals with advanced soft skills used an average of 4.4 different skills in a single, hour-long meeting.
- Last, 81% of participants who indicated they had hiring responsibilities as a part of their job said their hiring decisions were predominantly based on the soft skills an individual displayed during the interview.

With the early pieces of this research, I started to create a better way to learn, apply, and refine soft skills. After several prototypes, I arrived at what you see today as the Complete You Architecture™ or the CYA.

The three personal domains and 12 breakthrough skills are the most sought-after in the job market.

Image 2: The Complete You Architecture™

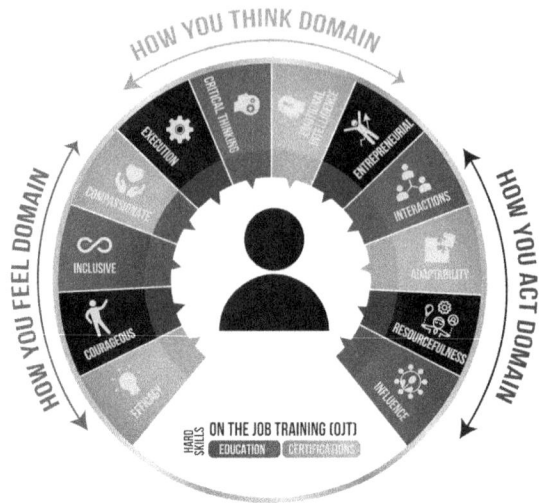

It did not take long to arrive at two separate conclusions about learning and applying soft skills. First, this is way too important of a topic to ignore. And second, no one, and I mean not a single college or organization, was doing anything new to improve how we learn soft skills and apply them in our professional careers.

Sure, universities and colleges will bury the conceptual definition of emotional intelligence or critical thinking in a course you might have taken. And I am confident that you quickly selected the correct answer on a multiple-choice exam. But that is usually the extent of soft skill learning you received if you attended college.

On top of that failed learning investment, your employer will spend thousands of dollars giving you quality on-the-job training specific to your role. Or they might even send you through a leadership academy with multiple gates or levels. But, what skills did you learn? How did that training and education help you develop the soft skills needed for your current role and future career?

Top 5 soft skills managers look for in employees:

- Critical Thinking
- Interactions
- Execution Mindset
- Resourcefulness
- Courage

Like many of you, I have plateaued once or twice in my career and rein-vented myself to get ahead. I have seen others advance faster than me, not because they were better educated, more intelligent, or more capable. They had soft skills that reflected a more polished professional at that time.

Soft skills are the most critical factors for advancing and achieving the success level you want. The brilliance of the CYA is that it links skills across three personal domains: how you think, feel, and act. Let me give you some examples:

Strong critical thinking skills don't help you much if you can't communi-cate and influence others to understand your point of view and inspire them to take action.

Being entrepreneurial and wanting to start a new venture won't work if you lack an execution mindset to take the first step, the self-efficacy to see it through to a positive conclusion, and the resourcefulness to bring it to life.

Emotional intelligence alone won't help you if you lack the courage to be a self-advocate and are unwilling to take a firm stance and show courage when needed.

The CYA isn't about learning a single soft skill. Still, instead, it is about creating a unique architecture that develops the right skills to balance each other and then learning how to link them together to do amazing things.

I have identified employers' four most sought-after skills for each of the three domains. The CYA consists of 12 breakthrough skills that all profes-sionals should aspire to master.

Warning

This skill training is not intended to replace formal education or on-the-job training. Still, it should be complementary and build off the knowledge foundation you have already earned.

Chapter 3
Introduction to the Three Domains

A DOMAIN IS a sphere of activity, influence, or knowledge.

For instance, the mindset is a domain in which you influence or take action over how you think. A person can learn how to improve any of the three domains that make up the CYA through the proper steps and steadfast commitment. This chapter will explore the three domains and why each is equally important to your career success.

Image 3: The Three Domains of the Complete You Architecture™

How You Think Domain

Most popular literature and models on soft skill development focus on the mindset. Which made my research into it the most complex of the three domains. Conventional thought would suggest that all 12 of the breakthrough skills which make up the CYA could, in theory, be part of the how you think domain.

For that reason, I had to better define the domains, how the skills are classified, and how you learn to link them.

The four breakthrough skills that make up the how you think domain are; critical thinking, emotional intelligence, execution, and entrepreneurial mindsets. These skills are unique in that they characterize how you think when you approach and respond to events in your daily life. More importantly, they reflect how you handle yourself when confronted with a new, unusual, or stressful situation.

How you respond during a heated discussion during a work meeting starts with how you think. Do you raise your voice back at the person who affronted you? Or do you show a high degree of emotional intelligence by keeping calm? Thus, you would be de-escalating the situation.

When you approach a new problem, do you have the critical thinking skills to seek information through inquisitive questioning and an execution mindset to take quick action to get things done?

How you think is frequently the starting point to creating skill links through the other two domains. As you learn to link skills and develop structures, you will often be drawn back to strengthening the four skills that make up the how you think domain.

How You Feel Domain

How you feel humanizes you through controlling your fear, acceptance, and perceived personal value. I refer to the four skills in this domain as your metaphorical heart. These skills influence how you internalize or outwardly express feelings when interacting with others.

The breakthrough skills that make up the how you feel domain are; compassion, inclusion, courage, and self-efficacy.

Do you demonstrate a willingness to take action towards self-improvement by building self-efficacy?

Are you compassionate in your daily life by helping those around you when you see an opportunity?

A great example of this is generating the courage to have a difficult conversation with your boss when you witness them have a lapse in judgment.

Are you inclusive by working to create an open, safe working environment for everyone? These efforts are all influenced by how you feel.

How You Act Domain

This third domain is the window you provide the world into your soft skills. Your outward projection of skills is how you demonstrate knowledge, mastery and receive feedback from those around you.

Simply put, it is how others view and perceive us. An outward projection through interaction is usually the only way an individual's soft skills can be evaluated, and a potential gap is identified. Thus, making this domain and its four skills crucial to success.

> *No Brainer*
> *Have you ever heard the phrase, "actions speak louder than words?" Well, this is it.*

Tying it back to the earlier point I made in Chapter 1, the how you act domain is often the building block you need to create a powerful, eye-catching resume. Take a quick moment to think about the last time you wrote or updated your resume. You highlighted actionable events and outcomes of actions you took. You highlighted the positive results of those actions. Once you entered the interview, the hiring manager probably asked open-ended behavioral questions to evaluate your skills through your past activities.

Here are a few interview questions I have used when assessing a candidate's potential:

- Tell me about a time you had to overcome a difficult challenge at work.
- When was the last time you took the initiative to try something new, and how did you approach it?
- How do you set personal development goals and ensure your direct manager helps you achieve them?

These interview questions are complex and require candidates to illustrate several soft skill links. More importantly, they need the candidate to show an action or outwardly projected behavior.

Then there is the flip side to this domain we must acknowledge. As observers peering into the windows of our peers, managers, and direct reports, we use this domain to evaluate their soft skills. It is also the main focus of our efforts when providing constructive feedback or coaching others. To illustrate this point:

A person can't claim to have emotional intelligence if their everyday interactions with others are emotional or aggressive.

A desire to be inclusive only becomes a reality when you take action to surround yourself with individuals who are different from you. Not only from the commonly accepted demographics perspective (gender, race, sexuality, etc.), but they should have contrasting backgrounds, experiences, and points of view.

We should agree that your outward projections are used to evaluate your soft skills. Failure to improve the skills that make up this domain could slow your career trajectory or prevent you from being as successful as you could be.

Through the CYA, you will learn that the first two domains, how you think and feel, must be linked to how you act. My research shows that more than three-quarters of all soft skills break down during the how you act domain. It also showed that a person's outwardly projected behaviors might not entirely reflect the hidden strengths of their skill set.

No Brainer
When applying and refining your newly learned skills, you must outwardly
project them so that others see an improvement.

Years ago, I worked with perhaps the most intelligent person I have ever met. He was a masterful critical thinker who could take action and execute at a very high level. His critical thinking and strong execution mindset helped him stand out amongst his peers early in his career. He quickly rose to senior vice president of a large sales division. But then his career plateaued. By achieving this level in his career, he found himself surrounded by other critical thinkers who also knew how to get things done.

Now the underdevelopment of other skills, particularly interactions and influencing others to action, caught up with him. It's been several years since he and I have worked together, but I know that this gifted leader, who had aspirations of one day being a CEO, is still in the same role as a vice president.

The moral of the story is that it takes more than just one or two soft skills to reach your full potential. You must learn to master several skills across all three domains and be able to link them to create a personal architecture that can be built upon as you progress in your career.

Chapter 4
What Makes the Complete You Architecture™ *Different?*

THE CYA IS one of a small handful of models, approaches, or methodologies focused on developing soft skills. Most are specific to leadership or coaching traits that organizations try to build within their workforce. While you might notice similarities with some of these models, the CYA is entirely different.

You need more than just a mindset.

First, let's discuss the increasing amount of attention spent on how an individual's mindset impacts their behavior. Yes, I agree that a person needs to have a growth mindset and be willing to take on new challenges when they arise. But then, what's next?

Social psychologist Carol Dweck introduced the Two Mindsets (fixed and growth) in 2006. Her best-selling book, *Mindset: The New Psychology of Success,* describes the two mindsets related to an individual's intelligence and where they believe it originates.

During a 2012 interview with the education publication OneDublin, Dr. Dweck describes the two mindsets this way:

"In a fixed mindset, students believe their basic abilities, intelligence, and talents are just fixed traits. They have a certain amount, and their goal is to look smart and never dumb. In a growth mindset, students understand that their talents and abilities can be developed through effort, good teaching, and persistence. They don't necessarily think everyone's the same or anyone can be Einstein, but they believe everyone can get smarter if they work at it."

Source: OneDublin.org interview. June 19, 2012.

It's a brilliant work that influenced millions worldwide and profoundly impacted how organizations approach employee and leadership development.

Image 4: Carol Dweck's Two Mindsets

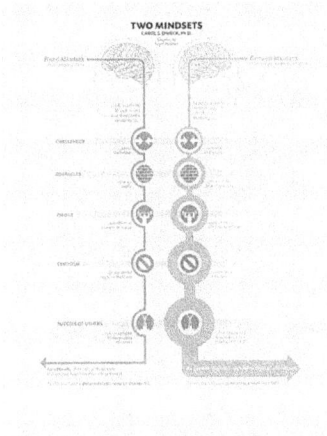

Source: Dweck, C. (2006). Mindset: The New Psychology of Success.

Notwithstanding its impact on society, my research into soft skills concluded that having a growth mindset does not always translate to success or positive outcomes when it is time to act.

An example of this came in the winter of 2019 when I observed an executive host a meeting of directors. During the meeting, she pitched a new idea to solve a lingering problem the team had faced for years. After several minutes of open discussion, I witnessed a significant shift in the mindset of those in attendance. The directors quickly went from doom and gloom to enthusiastic participants with a growth mindset.

The group collectively expressed that their challenge should not be a barrier. They were ready to take it on and finally have the persistence to succeed. The executive's elevated skills with interactions and influencing others turned the tide of the team discussion and convinced those in the room to embrace a growth mindset.

My engagement with this executive concluded about six months later. The problem was never resolved, and all efforts were abandoned again. The plan didn't succeed because it wasn't a good idea, or the motivation to fix it wasn't there. The team had demonstrated a growth mindset in that they embraced the challenge and were persistent in their action plan.

Instead, the collective team had failed in a few areas tied to other equally important skills that were not part of the mindset. First, they fell into the trap of not prioritizing this effort, which impacted their ability to execute it as they had planned. Next, they could not garner the resources across the broader organization to eliminate obstacles. And this was mainly due to not being able to influence others to take inspired action indirectly.

The lesson I took from this observation was that a person's mindset is only one of three equally critical personal domains. You need to be able to engage skills within all three domains; how you think, how you feel, and how you act, to truly achieve what you want.

Does leadership training prepare you for success?

In college, you might have been exposed to the conceptual knowledge of what a leader is. You could have learned about situational leadership, the path-goal theory, the leader-member exchange theory, or any other models. And if you followed a similar path as most college students, you joined the workforce.

Your employer then takes responsibility for your leadership development beyond a conceptual definition in what is typically a learn-as-you-go course after you become a people manager. As a manager, it is common-place that you may participate in an employer-hosted leadership academy or training workshop.

The main goals of employer-led training are usually related to teaching you some basic skills regarding communicating during difficult employee situations and how-to best coach your team to perform a specific task or job. A modern approach in these early leadership training is introducing a new model or acronym that is a simplified discussion guide when you are in coaching mode. During this training, you might be asked to practice by role-playing with a peer or two (because everyone loves awkward role-playing). At the end of the training, you are going to be sent back to your daily job, where you are expected to be able to use the newly learned model or acronym when it is time to have a crucial conversation with a team member. Good luck with that!

My intention is not to degrade the importance of leadership training. Instead, I am critical of both the arrogance and ignorance of the decision to try to train you on how to be an effective coach without actually teaching you an applicable soft skill.

Perhaps the root soft skill of self-reflection through emotional intelligence or how to take compassionate action towards a person you are coaching. Or, more importantly, this example, the self-efficacy, and courage needed to have a difficult conversation and see it through to a positive conclusion. Like most, these soft skills are ignored or avoided due to their difficulty in teaching and measuring effectiveness.

Before buying that next popular book, consider what you NEED to learn.

One last area I wish to draw a clear distinction with is another way we try to learn. Among the more popular mediums a person can turn to develop their soft skills are business or self-help books written by well-known executives or high-profile celebrities who bridge the gap between stardom and business success.

I recently was in my local bookstore looking for a good read before heading out on a much-needed vacation. I couldn't help but stop by the business section, where I noticed several recently authored books on leading with humility. While it is a beautiful notion, I found this humorous because our society idolizes leaders that most of us wouldn't consider humble.

To further make my point, in the same small section were books about Steve Jobs, Elon Musk, Donald J. Trump, Jeff Bezos, and Jack Welch, to name a few.

While indeed accomplished, you could never really describe any of these business leaders using the word humility. Nor could you or I ever repli-cate the skills and situations that have led to their achievement of fame and notoriety.

I love reading, and many books in my home library are on these leaders because of their entertainment value. But, for personal development purposes, I would suggest that instead of picking up a book that high-lights another person's greatness, I recommend that you focus on under-standing and developing the skills you need to fill your gaps. Find and strengthen the ones you need to meet the challenges of today and those tomorrow.

> *Tough Talk*
> *You will never be able to replicate the skills and situations that lead to the success of famous leaders. Don't try to be someone you are not.*

The CYA will undoubtedly enable you to be a more meaningful leader, coach, and manager without remembering a weird acronym or a prescribed model. You can accomplish this by learning the essential soft skills for your success. To improve, you must learn, apply, and refine these newly discovered skills as you develop your career.

Knowledge Check
Section 1

Grab a pen-paper, and answer the questions below to check your new knowledge from Section 1:

1. What are the two types of skills? What's the difference between them?
2. What type of skill is taught most often through on-the-job training?
3. The brilliance of the CYA is that it _____ skills across _____ domains.
4. What percentage of study participants said soft skills were a development gap within their organizations?
5. What is the most common way for people to evaluate their soft skills?
6. True or False: You can easily replicate the skills and situations that lead to the achievement of fame and notoriety of someone else.

Answer key: (1) Hard and Soft skills (2) Hard (3) links, three (4) 87% (5) Your outwardly projected behaviors found in the How You Act domain (6) False, you can NEVER replicate.

Section 2 - The Keys to Your Success

At the end of this section, you will:

- Get to know a simplified learning approach that makes mastering new skills quick and easy.
- Unlock the unbelievable power of consistency
- Become familiar with how to start linking soft skills across the three domains.
- Learn what a skill structure is and begin to create them as you learn the CYA.
- Be introduced to skill architecture and its four layers.

Quick Facts & Findings of Research Study

- Everyone, regardless of experience, education, and career level, can benefit from creating and expanding a personal skill architecture.
- Keeping a personal or professional journal is one of the most effective ways to improve consistency. Yet, only one out of 10 of us do this.

Top 5 reasons we struggle with consistency:

- Lack of patience
- The desire for instant gratification
- Lack of clarity and focus
- Not having supporting habits or triggers.
- Having an "all or nothing" mindset

Top 5 skill structures:

- Leadership
- Strategic Thinking
- Decision Making
- Communication
- Analytical skills

Top 5 sought-after soft skills:

- Critical Thinking
- Adaptability
- Courage
- Resourcefulness
- Emotional Intelligence

Chapter 5
The Ideal Learning Approach

IF YOU RECALL the introduction to this book, I mentioned that I had earned two master's degrees and even a doctorate. This means that I have been a college student for nearly 12 years. I have the student loan debt to prove it!

I also have a lot of learning experiences that worked great in college that I could share with you. I successfully listened to lectures, read expensive textbooks and peer-reviewed articles, used index cards for memorization, and set up study groups. These traditional learning methods prepared me well. I was successful because most college courses are about taking factual, conceptual, or procedural knowledge and remembering it on exam day. All we had to do as students were figure out how to learn in a manner that fit our needs at the time. The same could be said about high school classes.

I am not throwing shade at the promise of formal education, the millions of hard-working teachers, academics, and support staff that are the foundation of our learning. No, not at all. You will need this learning expertise to master the CYA.

Instead, I would like to draw your attention back to the 80 percent of young professionals (4 out of 5) who took part in my research study and reported that their education (college or high school) did not prepare them with the soft skills needed to be successful once they entered the workforce.

Part of the reason I believe that data was overwhelmingly skewed towards not being prepared is the types of knowledge predominantly taught in schools and colleges worldwide. It's challenging to turn factual, conceptual, and procedural knowledge about soft skills into outwardly projected behaviors (As discussed in Chapter 1).

The second reason I believe that data was overwhelmingly skewed is that our go-to approach to learning no longer applies to our post-formal education self. Meaning we need to rethink, or more appropriately, re-skill how we learn. The vast majority of us don't do this. Not because we can't shift our learning approach; we don't know that we need to. Therefore, the way we learn stays the same.

> *Tough Talk*
> *No one has ever told you that how you learn in school isn't ideal for doing so as a professional learner.*
>
> *Note: I use the term professional learner and not an adult learner. Adult learners returning to college or earning a work-related certificate need to apply the same approach they used in school. Being a professional learner is entirely different.*

The most significant difference between how we learned in school versus what we need now is that our goal for learning is no longer to pass an exam or a class. We now have to learn applicable skills (both hard and soft) that we can turn into sustainable behaviors and outcomes favorable to ourselves and employers.

Moreover, learning soft skills is unique because our environment influences our motivation to acquire new knowledge. Our learned soft skills derive primarily from either social or experiential learning.

Social learning is a motivational theory introduced in the 1940s by phycologist and Harvard Professor B.F. Skinner during a set of lectures on verbal behavior. The topic has been widely researched but gained additional notoriety in the late 1970s when Dr. Albert Bandura revised an earlier work to outline what has become known as the fundamental tenets of social learning theory.

Note: Dr. Albert Bandura was also responsible for introducing the self-efficacy theory. One of the twelve breakthrough skills of the CYA is taught in Chapter 16.

The five tenets of social learning theory are:

1. Learning is not purely behavioral; it is a *cognitive* process in a social context.
2. Learning can occur by observing a behavior *and* the consequences of the behavior (vicarious reinforcement).
3. Learning involves observation, extracting information from those observations, and making decisions about the performance of the behavior (observational learning or modeling). Thus, learning can occur without an observable change in behavior.
4. Reinforcement plays a role in learning but is not entirely responsible for education.
5. The learner is not a passive recipient of information. Cognition, environment, and behavior all mutually influence the learner's ability to absorb the information (reciprocal determinism).

Social learning significantly impacts the cognitive state of both adolescents and adults. The soft skills you have acquired and matured over the years as you attended primary school and possibly college were predominantly gained through social learning. You observed the desired behavior and imitated it until you received the positive reinforcement you were seeking. This behavior then became learned knowledge.

The second form of learning that shapes our motivation is experiential learning. As described by Patrick Felicia in the *Handbook of Research on Improving Learning and Motivation*, this is simply "learning through reflection on doing."

This theory was also a product of behavioral learning studies in the 1970s. It was first written about in its modern context by social psychologist David A. Kolb, Ph.D. As described by Dr. Kolb, the critical difference between experiential learning and what we might refer to as hands-on learning is reflection-on-action, which means that learning doesn't occur by doing but rather through the reflection that follows.

What did you learn if you tried something new but didn't reflect on its outcomes?

Note: Self-reflection is one of the root skills described in Chapter 10 on emotional intelligence.

The brief academic lesson on these two motivational learning theories is that we must completely rethink how we do it. That is why these two theories are the principal forces behind the learning approach recommended you apply during this workbook delete with your newly gained soft skill knowledge. And here is that approach…

Learn, apply, and refine

It is that simple to start mastering new skills. Yet, many of us struggle with turning time spent on learning and training as working adults into improved behaviors and favorable outcomes.

Image 5: The Ideal Learning Approach

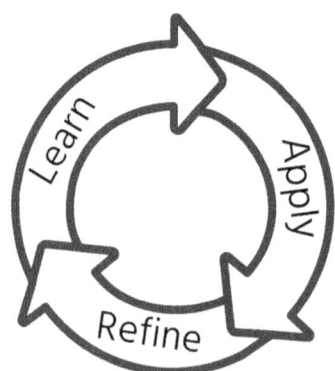

When was the last time you sat through a work-related training seminar or read a book in the hopes of taking away a valuable nugget of new knowledge that could apply to your everyday life?

Did you gain anything beyond understanding the concepts, principles, theories, or models presented (i.e., conceptual knowledge)? The brutal truth is that most of us rarely take any applicable lessons from the time we spend learning.

In contrast, there are many theories as to why so little of our investment in training and learning results in little to no improvement; the consensus is the lack of follow-through on turning the acquired knowledge into new ways of thinking and working. Thus it renders the learning exercise fatally flawed.

For that reason, the learning approach I recommend focuses your efforts on three distinct parts:

Learn

Part one is to learn. Which is what we are accustomed to with the intake of new knowledge through conventional or unconventional channels. We have all experienced learning through formal education, obtaining professional certifications, and on-the-job training. These different channels provide us with the observations, experiences, and feedback we need to build a foundation of knowledge. This is the expertise that you already have from your formal education.

Apply

The second part is to apply the learnings you have just obtained. Applying your learnings to immediate use is crucial to turning them into behaviors and habits. The goal of any professional learning endeavor is to be able to transfer it into an outcome that improves the current status quo. That can not be accomplished when learning is not applied.

Warning
The application of learning is usually the breakdown because no follow-through occurs. If the learnings are not applied, then the personal gains you

could have achieved are forfeited. Not lost, but rather given up until you
decide to use them.

Refine

The third part of this learning approach is to refine your application of the knowledge you have acquired. During refining your applied learnings, you experience actual personal growth and development through self-reflection. No matter how you learn, almost all of what you take in is often too generalized and does not fully relate to your situation, environment, or challenges.

That does not mean that learning wastes time or effort. It would help if you refined it to make it your own and achieve the desired outcomes.

How did you get better at riding a bike when you were younger? Or throwing a ball? Or swimming?

You learned how to do it. You applied that learning. And then you refined it until it became second nature. Hence the saying, "it's like riding a bike." Meaning that once you have learned, you will never forget it.

Thus, you have come full circle. You learn, apply, and refine continuously until you attain mastery.

Chapter 6
Your Personal Super Power

WHILE OBTAINING my undergraduate degree a couple of decades ago, my roommate decorated his side of our two-person dorm room with a few inspirational posters. These eye-catching depictions of vast mountain ranges offered everyone who observed them a dose of motivation with a catchy phrase or quote. Of the three that took up his side of the room, the middle poster is the only one I can remember.

Over a darkened blue mountain, the white lettering scribed out: "Consistency is the key to success."

It might have been the preoccupations of being a 21-year-old college student, but that poster never made sense to me at the time. It was not until I got into my thirties and became an executive, later a strategy consultant, and eventually a parent that it started to resonate. Consistency is the key to success.

Consistency of thought, feelings, and actions are performance multipliers for soft skill development. The more consistent you are across the three domains when performing your newly acquired skills, the greater your likelihood of rising above and standing out among peers.

> *Warning:*
> *The most common way the learning process breaks down is inconsistent in applying your new skills.*

Here are some of the known benefits of being consistent in your thoughts, feelings, and actions:

- Consistency accelerates self-improvement by reinforcing new knowledge.
- Consistency allows you to develop self-efficacy, one of the 12 breakthrough skills in the CYA (Chapter 17)
- Consistency gets you noticed at work because leaders love an employee they can count on.
- Consistency is a motivator because you are getting noticed, assigned higher priority tasks, and building trust with influential leaders.
- Consistency helps you create and strengthen relationships.
- Consistency improves your career trajectory and opens doors.

I used the word "consistency" with each benefit description to best illustrate the point. Here are three ways to build up this vital superpower:

Use a daily journal and plan

If, like so many others, you struggle with being consistent, I strongly recommend that you start to use a daily journal during the first 30 days after you complete this workbook.

The consistency you achieve by using daily journal conditions you to self-reflect on the learning approach described in Chapter 5. It also provides an outlet to capture moments of refinement or lessons learned to work towards genuinely mastering these skills. Additional benefits of journaling are strengthening two emotional intelligence root skills by becoming more self-aware and improving your situational awareness as you apply and refine your new skills. You will find more on both these tools in the next chapter.

Win with incremental improvements

A second way to improve consistency is to focus on incremental improvements. In other words, you strengthen a single skill at a time so that all your attention and effort are making improvements in a single area.

Tough Talk
You shouldn't expect to complete this workbook and be able to master all 12
of the skills in the CYA quickly. Soft skill learning does not occur with huge
gains but with incremental improvements.

Three quick points on incremental progress:

1. Remember that many small steps equal a considerable leap (often with less effort).
2. Ever heard the phrase, "if it were easy, then everyone would be doing it."
3. The learning process breaks when individuals don't apply or refine new knowledge (Chapter 5). You will have to apply and refine your new skills incrementally to improve.

As part of my newfound career as an educator of soft skills, I consult with companies to introduce the CYA and teach it to their leaders and teams through workshops, leader development sessions, and personal assignments. Inevitably, I reach the lesson on the consistency I am sharing with you now. In almost every one of the workshops or leader development sessions I have led, someone in the room will ask, "Isn't it better for us to work on all the skills simultaneously?"

The answer is always "no." This usually opens up a brief discussion as to why not focusing on all the skills at once is the best way to learn the CYA or any new knowledge you acquire as a professional. I am adamant that you focus on incremental improvements through one skill at a time because that ties back into the benefits of consistency outlined above.

Most of us can't be consistent when trying to apply several new skills simultaneously. Furthermore, if we can't consistently apply multiple new skills, we will lose motivation because we do not see the gains we want. Instead, you should be laser-focused on a single skill and strengthen it through daily application and refinement.

No Brainer
Most commonly accepted research suggests that a person can create muscle
memory, or the unconscious use of new knowledge, between 60 to 75 days

after learning it. That might sound like a long time, but in the grand scheme of your career, it's a drop in the ocean. Psst… daily planning and journaling can speed this up.

Get comfortable with failure

The third way to improve consistency in applying your new skills is to learn how to fail. We are all afraid of failing for any number of reasons. Most relate to our fear of looking bad or being worried that our work environment isn't safe and our manager won't allow for rapid failure and learning.

I have rarely seen a manager not support an employee trying something new with the time they need to work through it and fail along the way. Most managers encourage this behavior and want to see more of it from their teams. A good leader isn't interested in your failure or the number of times it occurs. They want to know how you apply the lessons learned from failing. They want to see how you handle trying something new and not being successful at it with your first attempt. They want to see you try and try again when things don't go how you want them to.

It's the human in us all.

As a parent, you teach your child how to ride a bike. They're not going to get it on their first try. They fall, and you encourage them to get up and try again. Offer a few words of encouragement and some tips on how to pedal faster or not to turn so sharply. Then they go again with you, running along the side, holding onto the bike seat until it's time to let them go. But, even the second time, they fail shortly after you let go. And again and again, until eventually, they go a long distance. You both rejoice in excitement! Not just for the accomplishment but because they didn't give up when they fell and skinned their knee or elbow. They got up and kept trying until they succeeded.

Managers are human too. They would prefer you to try something new and fail along your way to success rather than for you to try and give up immediately.

In Chapter 11, you will learn the five ways to fail as part of the entrepreneurial mindset. Here is a sneak peek:

1. Quickly - The quicker you identify failure, the quicker you can learn and apply those learnings.
2. Cheaply - Don't rush to scale, invest, or celebrate until you know you have failed for the last time.
3. Frequently - Because you move closer to success with each failure.
4. Elegantly - If we accept failure, we must accept it as part of the learning process.
5. Safely - The number one reason individuals don't take risks at work and in their careers is that they don't have the feeling of safety in their environment.

Harnessing the power of consistency in your application and refinement of new skills will accelerate your development. These three ways can improve your ability to be consistent in thought, feeling, and action.

Tough Talk
Consistency can either be your superpower or it can be your kryptonite. The choice is yours.

Chapter 7
Learning How to Link Skills

LINKING OCCURS when you apply more than one domain or soft skill to progress a thought or an activity toward a conclusion. Below is a quick scenario that will illustrate how skills can be linked.

You are a team leader, running a meeting to plan out next month's workload, and as you sit there listening to the room, you start to notice that the six other people look, think, and have the same professional background as you. This isn't bad, but many benefits come with a diverse team that you might miss out on.

These benefits include:

- Increased job satisfaction
- Higher productivity
- More creativity and innovation
- Accelerated speed to transform and improve individual adaptability
- Higher employee engagement and morale
- Better customer satisfaction
- Stronger employee retention
- Improved revenue and profitability growth

As you process this realization, you decide to speak up. You gently point out your observation to the team and ask them their thoughts. You look at each team member across the table and ask, "Would we benefit from improving the diversity of thought in our monthly meetings, and should we start to include other teammates?"

At that moment, you have linked a minimum of five soft skills:

1. Emotional intelligence with the realization of the lack of diversity on your team.
2. Inclusion by wanting to change the team's dynamics.
3. A second inclusion root skill is demonstrated by you asking the team their thoughts.
4. The courage to speak up.
5. Use this frequent interaction (monthly meeting) with your team to maximize an opportunity.

Image 6: Example of the skill link for the above scenario

But what happens next to make this effort a reality and improve the team's diversity and inclusion during this meeting?

Maybe you could apply critical thinking skills in identifying potential knowledge gaps on your team and the possible team members to fill those gaps. You will also need to link an execution mindset to bring the team's plan to life and to take action.

These are just two more examples of soft skills that would need to be linked for this example. As you can imagine, not having one of these crucial skills could be why the plan doesn't come to fruition and your team doesn't capitalize on the benefits of improved diversity.

Image 7: Additional two skills being linked

While this example used the complex topic of diversity to illustrate how skills can be linked during a team meeting, the opportunity to link skills is often less convoluted. You will see a few more examples during this chapter that will help you better understand skill linking. But first, let's talk about how to create a link.

Throughout my research, I identified four ways a person can learn to link skills to progress a thought or an activity toward a conclusion:

Recognize cognitive triggers

The first way is to understand and start to recognize cognitive triggers. You would realize a mental trigger as that inner voice that speaks up or that gut feeling you can't shake when you feel something more is needed.

Perhaps the best example of one is when you hastily type out an email, and midway through it, you start to ask yourself, "Should I send this?" That is an example of a cognitive trigger we can all relate to.

Here is what that skill link would look like if you recognized a trigger and took positive action to your hastily typed email:

Image 8: First cognitive trigger example

Another example is when you find yourself sitting in a meeting with the urge to speak up in support or opposition to a topic building inside you. Again, this is a cognitive trigger.

> *No Brainer*
> *I used the decision icon from flowchart symbols intentionally. You cannot just recognize the cognitive trigger; rather, you need to decide to take action. Yes, action can be to continue despite the trigger, or it could be to take an alternative course.*

Image 9: Second cognitive trigger example

As you look at these two everyday scenarios, it is essential to point out the skill that follows the trigger. I refer to this as the "pivot skill."

You are fired up while writing a blistering email response when you recognize a trigger. What do you do next? If you ignore the trigger, you don't pivot and continue on the course to send the email. But, if you acknowledge the trigger, you redirect using the next skill. This example requires self-awareness not to send a blistering email response. Self-awareness is a root skill for emotional intelligence. Much more on that later.

You will recognize more triggers as you learn, apply, and refine the breakthrough skills that make up the CYA. More importantly, you will learn how to "pivot" when one occurs.

Utilize both a daily journal and a daily plan on a page

The second way to learn to link skills is to utilize a daily journal and a daily plan when preparing for a critical moment. Starting with the latter, planning the soft skills you want to use during a day, in a particular meeting, or when interacting with a specific individual might sound odd. Still, it can be a very influential factor during your learning process.

When you start your day off or prepare for a meeting by identifying where you have the opportunity to use a newly learned skill, you are more likely to apply it and do it well.

Journaling, or the act of reflection-on-action, is equally important. Much research has shown that writing down your thoughts, feelings, and progress toward a goal keeps you focused and improves your chances of success.

Like most, I have needed to diet as I have gotten older. I could eat anything I wanted up to the age of 40. Then my metabolism slowed down, work got more stressful, and I had less time to exercise—the trifecta for weight gain.

Over the years, I have tried many trending and popular diets; Atkins, Keto, and so forth. But the one that I was most successful with was Weight Watchers. If you are unfamiliar with the program, it's a lifestyle change in that they teach you how to eat better without giving up all the foods you love.

The support materials I would use to plan and record my daily eating habits were most beneficial to me. Not to get too personal, but when I started Weight Watchers in 2016, I weighed slightly more than 250 lbs. It took me about nine months to reach my goal weight of 190lbs. A 60-pound difference! The best part is that I have maintained that weight since I reached it. While I still don't utilize a daily eating journal, the lessons learned by writing it habitually have conditioned me to consider what I am eating throughout the day.

The simple and proven approach to meal journaling has made Weight Watchers very successful and undoubtedly contributes to why the company has been around since 1963. Not to mention it was a significant contributor to my successful weight loss. Similarly, your learning experience here should also include proper planning and the use of a journal to reflect on your success and struggles as you apply and refine your skills.

Focus your efforts on performance-magnifying skills

The third way to learn how to link soft skills is to focus your efforts on performance-magnifying skills. Every position or job you have ever had, or will have, requires a specific skill set to be successful.

I have found that learners who select one or two skills related to their current job to focus on strengthening are six times more successful than those who try to learn, apply, and refine a soft skill they don't use frequently.

There are two ways to approach identifying performance magnifying skills:

The first is to identify skills that are part of the work you dislike or that causes you stress or anxiety. Think for a minute about your current job.

- What aspects or activities of your job do you dislike the most?
- What are the ones that you know you need to do better?
- Next, what are the soft skills most related to those listed above?

Of the skills you have just identified, which one or two would be the most important to learn and strengthen?

Perhaps you are a sales professional struggling with planning your weekly schedule or route. In the past, you just woke up and went to work, letting your day unfold as things came up. If you have ever sold before, you know that's not a great way to be successful long-term. So, as a sales professional, you consider the skills that are part of the task of planning out your weekly call schedule, then you might land on one of the following skills:

- Critical thinking to better know where your most significant sales opportunities are each day
- Entrepreneurial mindset to take ownership over your work and sales territory
- Execution mindset to set aside dedicated time each Friday afternoon to plan the next week
- Resourcefulness in reaching out to a peer you know is good at planning.
- Self-efficacy to start the task and see it through to a positive conclusion week after week

In identifying these skills, you conclude that you don't know enough about how to best plan your week. So, you make it a point to be resourceful and contact a co-worker who can help you.

Ultimately, you gain the knowledge you need to succeed and then turn to the next skill you need to apply in planning your weekly schedule. That could also be any of the ones listed above. You have begun linking skills to a job task or activity you dislike. As with most things, it will become easier as we learn how to do it, apply it, and refine it to meet our unique situation.

If you are unsure how to select or identify the right skills to work on, that's no problem. This leads us to the second way to focus on performance-magnifying skills.

You chose this workbook to help you learn new soft skills. You had at least one skill in mind for what you wanted to improve. What is it? That is an excellent place to start too.

If you are stuck with selecting a skill to focus on, that's okay too. Complete this workbook and learn the skills that are part of the CYA. There is plenty of time to identify one of them you can strengthen as you go through this workbook.

> *No Brainer*
> *Utilizes all three of these methods to learn how to link soft skills together. Using all three will drastically improve your learning experience and accelerate the speed at which you start to see an improvement.*

Be on the lookout for natural positive connections

An element of skill learning that will become more apparent as you progress through this workbook is the natural connections between specific skills. Like all connections, some are positive, and others can be conflicting.

Positive connections occur with skill links when two skills complement each other. For example, courage and adaptability form a strong relationship because it takes courage to be willing to change or transform yourself without being pressed to do it.

Here are a few of the most common positive connections you will find with the CYA:

- Emotional intelligence and compassion
- Execution mindset and self-efficacy
- Entrepreneurial mindset and resourcefulness
- Interactions and influence
- Courage and interactions
- Compassion and inclusion

There are several more positive connections in the CYA where the skills complement each other.

Next are the conflicting connections that occur when skills are in natural conflict. Perhaps the best example of two skills being at odds with each other is emotional intelligence and courage.

Too often, I have witnessed individuals stay silent when a moment of courage is needed because they have been trained or conditioned, emphasizing emotional intelligence. Most consider saying nothing as a form of mature emotional intelligence. This is especially true with a young professional who cares more about showing control over their emotions than showing courage's raw emotional aspect.

Inclusion and influence are two other skills that can be in conflict. This is because when a person first starts gaining influence in the workplace, their natural tendency is not to be inclusive so they hoard the influential power they have gained.

Here are a few of the most common conflicting connections:

- Emotional intelligence and courage
- Inclusion and influence
- Entrepreneurial mindset and compassion
- Execution mindset and adaptability

The conflict between skills is natural and won't be harmful as you learn to balance and apply the skill most applicable to a particular scenario.

The good news is that you will start to recognize these relationships as you apply and refine the skills that are part of your architecture.

Chapter 8
How to Create Skill Structures

NOTHING IS MORE critical to your architecture than creating and maturing the individual skill structures you will need for success today and tomorrow. At the end of this chapter, you will know how to create structures and will be able to build them as you learn the 12 breakthrough skills that make up the CYA.

So, what is a skill structure?

As I worked through the early iterations of the CYA, I knew I was on to something special. But, as with most great ideas, it would only be extraordinary if I could convince you it was. To do that, I had to give it structure.

A structure is a house, building, tower, bridge, and other artificial physical object. But, a structure is also the polymer double-helixes of human DNA, the chemical makeup of medication, or the arrangement of words that make this a chapter within a book.

A structure can be both physical and also exist in the abstract.

I define a skill structure as the intentional arrangement of soft skills as part of a more complex construct.

> *Important Note: A skill structure and links are different. As you recall from Chapter 7, a link is the application of skills to progress a thought or an*

activity toward a conclusion. At the same time, a skill structure is not thought or activity-centric.

If that sounds confusing or too academic, it is not. Let me explain this concept with a simple example. To do so, let's start with a few quick questions:

What is leadership?

How would you define it?

What traits or characteristics do great leaders have?

The Oxford Languages dictionary defines leadership as the act of leading a group of people or an organization. A second definition is a state or position of being a leader. However, leadership or being called a leader isn't always the same for everyone. If we surveyed a hundred people, no two individuals would have the exact definition of leadership. And that is ok. Let me make the point more clearly.

Here are a few examples of modern and historical leaders who led a group of people or organizations and thus, by definition, are leaders.

19th Century Leaders

- Abraham Lincoln, 16th President of the United States (1861 to 1865)
- Napoleon Bonaparte, Emperor of the French (1804 to 1814)

Religious Leaders

- Mother Teresa, Saint Teresa of Calcutta (died: 1997)
- Billy Graham, American Evangelist & ordained Southern Baptist Minister (died: 2018)

Recent American Politics

- Barack Obama, 44th President of the United States (2009 to 2017)
- Donald J. Trump, 45th President of the United States (2017 to 2021)

Looking at these individuals, you can see that leadership or being a leader can mean drastically different things. These examples have entirely different characteristics, traits, and skill sets. Yet, they are all leaders by definition, and I chose these leaders because they are in sharp contrast.

This gets me to my point.

The challenge that academia and on-the-job training programs have is that leadership is taught using broad strokes based on a flawed understanding of what defines a leader at that very moment in time and within the preset boundaries of an organization. Organizations and colleges try to develop leaders using conceptual or procedural knowledge without teaching the root skills that would make an individual a great or even a good leader.

Root skills such as active listening, self-reflection, asking questions, empathy, prioritizing tasks, and many others are not developed during the early stages of learning because they are only taught as conceptual knowledge. For instance, self-reflection is defined in lessons on emotional intelligence, but most still don't know how to do it.

The company you work for is spending a lot of money, time, and energy telling you that leading with empathy is a good thing and you should do it. But what does that mean? You know you should ask more questions during team meetings, but what are the good questions you should be asking?

> *Tough Talk*
> *The underdevelopment of root skills is why many professionals lack the soft skills they need to succeed in their current jobs. Remember, 4 out of 5 young professionals say that their education did not prepare them with the soft skills vital to their success in the workforce. That's 80 percent!*

This brings us back to the topic at hand. Leadership is a complex construct comprising numerous soft skills that must be evolved and interchanged over time. It is a structure.

The best way to understand your skills structures and develop them is to draw them out. By drawing them out, you can identify where you have strengths and areas of opportunity for growth. Each of your structures has three different components that make up its blueprint (See Image 10):

Image 10: Three elements of a skill structure

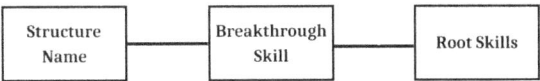

1. The structure name identifies the construct and the correlating skills that make it up. Each structure will only have one name (i.e., leadership, giving presentations, talent development).
2. The breakthrough skill(s) directly follow(s) the structure name and are pulled from the 12 breakthrough skills that are part of the CYA. These are the core skills for the structure. Note: every structure will have multiple breakthrough skills (see Image 11).
3. The last component outlines the root skills of each breakthrough skill. For example, self-reflection is a root skill of emotional intelligence. Radical candor is a root skill of courage. As with the breakthrough skills in your structure, you can have multiple root skills (See Image 11).

At 22 years old, I became a people manager for the first time and was responsible for a team of six individuals. In leading a team of grocery stockers, I needed to know how to execute tasks, influence others to perform their work, and interact positively with customers.

Fast forward 20 years, as a partner with one of the world's largest consulting firms, I had to use all the skills I mentioned in drastically different ways, plus a few additional skills. I had to show compassion, self-efficacy, critical thinking, and an entrepreneurial mindset to solve client needs and grow the 60-person practice I was responsible for. In both cases, by definition, I was a leader.

The skill structure I required to lead that team of stockers at my local grocery store was entirely different from the structure I needed to lead a practice of over 60 international consultants.

Worse, the formal training I received for both positions was almost identical. The content was presented in PowerPoint, the training was a full day long, it was formal classroom learning using a couple of role-plays, and even the post-training evaluation was the same (which there was none). This generic, company-led leadership training was focused too much on transferring useless conceptual knowledge.

Have you had similar experiences?

So like you, I had to learn the soft skills I needed to be successful on my own, typically through trial and error. Hence, I was motivated to become a researcher of soft skills and begin the journey of better understanding soft skills, which led to the creation of the CYA.

> *Tough Talk*
> *The soft skills you have today are not sufficient for you to achieve your true potential.*

The topic of leadership is not alone in this misguided attempt to educate the masses. Ever been asked if you are a strategic thinker? Or how you make decisions? How do you resolve a conflict with a peer? These are all examples of the many different skill structures that exist.

List of common skill structures:

- Leadership
- Strategic Thinking
- Decision Making
- Communication
- Analytical skills
- People Management & Development
- Ethics
- Creativity
- Selling
- Problem-Solving

> *Note: There is a near-limitless number of different structure possibilities. Some are easily recognizable, like these 10; others are hidden from sight. Or they could be specific to a job or career level or could be something entirely new that you create on your own. These are your structures; you have complete freedom to be creative. Just be sure to include the skills of the CYA as your breakthrough elements.*

Suppose you want to be a better leader. Become a strategic thinker capable of making quick, informed, and accurate decisions. Know how to resolve conflicts and coach a team of individuals to perform at their highest level. Then, you need to learn the soft skills that make up each of these skill structures. As you progress in your career, your skill structures will need to be scaled and rebuilt to meet your emerging needs at that moment in time. See my two different leadership skill structures below.

Image 11: The left skill structure is from my retail leadership experience. The right one is from my time as a Partner at a consulting firm.

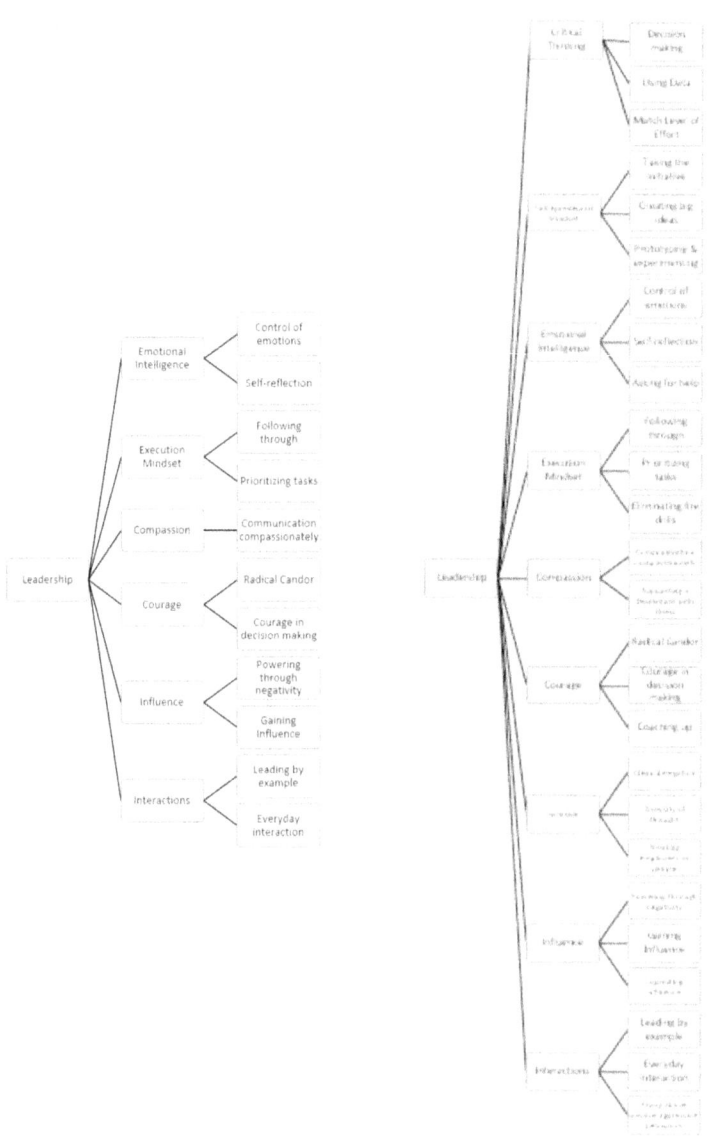

How to start creating your skill structures

Having been introduced to the definition of a skill structure, its different components, and seeing my examples of leadership, I am sure your mind is racing with different experiences and skills you could list. This is fantastic, but don't get too far ahead because you still need to learn the 12 breakthrough skills that make up the CYA and the root skills presented in each lesson.

Structures and how to create them are being introduced in this early chapter not for you to start creating them immediately, but rather from the experiences I have heard others have when starting. Much of the feedback I have received when individuals begin to develop structures is that they either jump in and start immediately or wait until after they learn each of the 12 skills to get started. Both present unique challenges:

1. If you start too early, how can you create a structure without learning the breakthrough skills of the CYA?
2. How can you ensure you capture all the relevant skills for each structure if you wait?

For this reason, the best approach to start creating your very first structures is a "add as you learn" plan. The steps described below are the easiest way to identify and create each, but the best technique is to start a list of potential structures (steps 1 - 3), and then as you advance through this workbook, add each breakthrough and root skill that are part of it.

> *No Brainer*
> *By adding as you learn, you self-reflect while the new knowledge you have gained is fresh. This makes for an ideal learning experience.*

To create your structures, follow these steps:

1. Identify the job duties and responsibilities you have or do as part of your job today
2. List the specific activities or ways you think or work for each of these duties

3. For each activity in step 2, list the potential skill structure names that you frequently use
4. Select one of the structure names you wrote down in step 3 and start to list the breakthrough skills from the CYA that are part of it
5. Move to the third element in your structure and list the root skills that are part of each breakthrough skill

Next, make sure to choose the tool that's best for you.

When I first started creating my structures, I used pencil and paper. It is a great way to quickly jot ideas down, mark revisions, and make fast corrections. As I learned how to build structures, I began using Microsoft PowerPoint. This made it easier for me to add or update structures. I still love putting pencil to paper and later transferring the structure into a file.

To do this, I use a simple SmartArt in PowerPoint, found in the Insert tab, and then choose a horizontal hierarchy. Doing this allows me to add the three distinct levels and more boxes as needed to show my breakthrough and root skills (Image 10). The image of my two leadership structures above was built using PowerPoint.

No Brainer
Microsoft has many easy-to-use tutorials if you have never made a hierarchy in PowerPoint. Visit https://support.microsoft.com/.

If you use Apple's Keynote, at the time of this writing, they do not currently offer a solution to build a hierarchy quickly. Instead, you will be adding shapes and lines for connectors. While not difficult, it is a little more time-consuming.

The cognitive process of identifying and building your structures will help you assess your known skill strengths that you are capable of applying and those that need further attention. The scope of this exercise isn't only to list what you can do but to find gaps and areas of opportunities with the structures you need to be successful.

No Brainer
I strongly recommend you start by listing the structures you use and then complete this workbook. As you learn the 12 skills that make up the CYA,

you can expand to include the breakthrough and root skills that make up your structures.

Collapsing skill structures into skill cards

At the end of this workbook, you will build your architecture in Chapter 22. The first step you will complete is to collapse your structures into cards. The skill card simplifies the view and allows you to place it into your architecture. Image 12 uses the leadership structure from my retail days to illustrate how a complex construct gets reduced or collapsed into a skill card.

To create architecture, you must collapse the details of a structure into a skill card so that you can view multiple ones simultaneously. This allows you to place cards in the correct layer easily, but more importantly, it gives you a high-level view of your architecture.

Image 12: Skill structure to card view

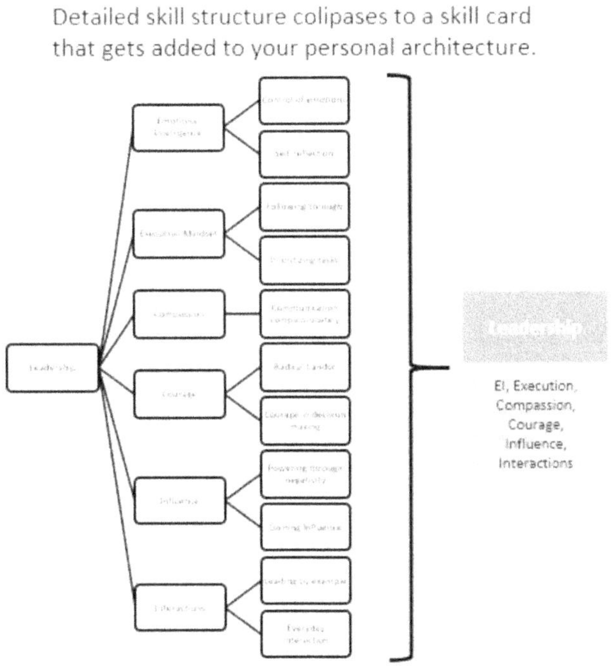

Detailed skill structure colipases to a skill card that gets added to your personal architecture.

Leadership

EI, Execution, Compassion, Courage, Influence, Interactions

Chapter 9
What is Skill Architecture

THE WORD ARCHITECTURE provokes images of immaculate buildings or structures praised for their beauty, functionality, and contribution to human society during historical periods.

Depending on your tastes, the word might conjure images of Modernism or Postmodernism skyscrapers like the Burj Khalifa in Dubai, The Shard in London or the modern expressionist design of the Sydney Opera House completed in 1973.

You might prefer the Art-Deco icons of the early 20th century; The Empire State Building and the Chrysler Building in New York City. Still too modern?

Then like me, your architectural taste might be more historical and reside in the Neo-classical period, which produced the United States Capitol Building and the Belvedere Palace in Vienna. Another of my favorite periods, Gothic architecture, gave us Notre Dame Cathedral in Paris, Salisbury Cathedral in England, and St. Patrick's Cathedral in Dublin.

Each of these brilliant architectural styles was heavily influenced by the society of their time and, in return, influenced our appreciation of buildings' social, functional, and technical aspects.

In designing and constructing each, the architects had to scrutinize many considerations that applied to the exterior beauty we adore and the inner complexities that make them work as intended. Why build Notre Dame if no one could attend mass? Why build the 2,722' Burj Khalifa if you can't reach the office space, hotel, shopping, and residences that make up its upper floors? All were built for the property owner to generate a profit.

The monumental challenge in designing and constructing architectural masterpieces is finding the proper balance between function and value to society. Similarly, as you create your skill architecture, you must balance the role and importance of soft skills.

To accomplish this, you will need to start viewing architecture using its second meaning as defined by the Oxford Languages Dictionary; "a complex or carefully designed structure."

No Brainer
Remember, a structure is an arrangement between elements or parts of something complex.

In Chapter 8, I asserted that the intentional arrangement of soft skills creates a structure (leadership, communication, decision-making, etc.). You need architecture to balance the function and value of your skill structures.

Thus, the combination of all your skill structures is your architecture!

Before we discuss the layout, layers of your architecture, and how you create one, allow me to show you mine as an example:

Image 13: My skill architecture (updated 2022)

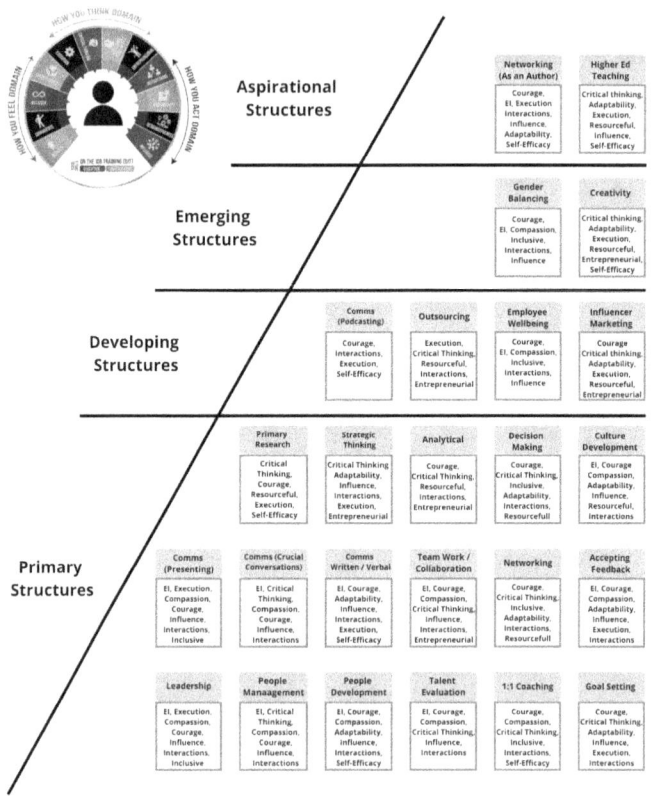

Architecture is a snapshot in time. Mine was updated in January 2022 to illustrate the skill structures I apply in my current role and those structures I am developing. The architectural design is intentional so that the layout illustrates the balance between the skills you have matured and those under further development. This is the balance between function and value.

No Brainer

My complete (historical) architecture has about two times more Primary Structures than displayed in the above image. Since architecture views the current state, I only show those skills I actively use in my foundation. As you build your architecture, you will also have several mature structures, which should be captured in holistic architecture.

Get to Know the Different Architectural Layers

Architecture is a complex, carefully designed set of skill structures that are both static and dynamic. Static because once you have matured or mastered a soft skill, it is transferable across your career. It is dynamic because you are in the growth zone and constantly learn and influence your ecosystem.

To illustrate the relationship between static structures and dynamic ones, each is arranged into four different layers. These layers enable you to create a logical balance between function and value.

Image 14: Architecture Template

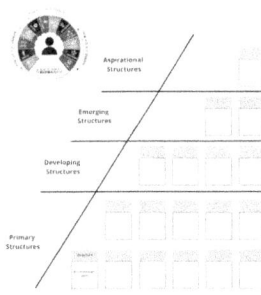

Use the large template in Chapter 22 to create your Complete You Architecture as you complete this workbook.

Here are the four layers that make up an architecture (starting at the bottom):

Layer 1: Primary Structures

The best way to think about your primary structures is that these are the ones you are good at. You have developed high self-efficacy (Chapter 16) and can perform them with near unconscious effort. Thus, they are transferable across time, roles, and your career.

No Brainer

As you create your personal architecture, ideally, you will want to focus on performance-magnifying skills that are part of the structures you are or should be applying as part of your current job.

An accomplished teacher can establish classroom management (a career-specific skill structure) with his students and maintain it throughout the year with little effort. This structure is then applied at the offset to each school year with different classes. An established graphic designer can listen openly to constructive feedback and receive revisions on their work without feeling personally assaulted. As part of their job, they might have multiple projects that will be reviewed daily or weekly. These examples are primary structures that illustrate a high level of maturity and are transferable.

Note: A career-specific skill structure applies to a particular profession. For instance, we know that communication is a skill structure that applies to almost all jobs but communicating medical instructions during a high-stakes surgery is a career-specific structure.

Layer 2: Developing Structures

The second layer should be easy to understand. These are the structures and related soft skills that you are working to improve. You have identified them as opportunities to strengthen and learn how to apply and link each across the three domains.

Structures stay in this layer of your architecture until you have demonstrated mastery. Once this is achieved, it is moved down to your primary layer. A second way to remove a structure from this layer is to make the conscious decision that it is no longer functional or adds value to your professional development. This is a simple form of prioritization for the soft skills you are learning.

Notice that in my architecture, I have communication in both my primary and delete-developing layers. It is widespread to have the same structure at different layers due to maturity levels with the individual soft skills that are part of that complex construct. Communicating an idea during a presentation or live webinar is a primary structure. But, doing it in my podcast, where I can't see the audience and respond to their engagement, body language, and questions, requires me to develop this structure further, hence, why it is included in my developing layer.

Layer 3: Emerging Structures

The third layer in your architecture is the structures emerging as part of your ecosystem. These are driven by changes in your work, leadership, or career. Like developing structures, these are ones that you are working to improve. However, the difference with emerging structures is that they are not self-identified. Instead, forces outside your control are influencing your motivation.

The best example is how work shifted from in-person to remote for millions of us in 2020 due to Covid-19. Due to an outside influence, we quickly had to learn new skills and create new structures while trying not to let productivity slip. If you were one of the millions of employees across the globe that went from working every day in a co-located location to working remotely, what new structures did you have to develop?

And are those skill structures now part of your primary layer?

The move from co-located to remote work was extreme. We had little to no choice in the level of effort we would put forth in learning, applying, and refining the new skills required to be successful during the pandemic. Most of us were highly motivated because our jobs depended on our ability to learn and perform these new skills. But what if an emerging structure was less dire and had more flexibility in your level of motivation?

In the early 2000s, I was a newly promoted sales manager leading a team of eight. After about six months in the role, a new vice president was hired for the region I was part of. This individual was highly motivated to make a positive impact, so within his first 90 days, he put several new initiatives in motion. One was developing the front-line sales managers' ability to have tough conversations with their team members. This VP made a substantial investment by hiring a third-party consultant group to teach us how to use a modeled approach.

The group, Inside Out Development (https://www.insideoutdev.com/), trained more than 30 managers over a three-day workshop. We were taught a model to apply when having crucial conversations, given tons of support materials, and participated in role plays while we were in person. At the end of the week, we were asked to take our new knowledge back to our teams and use it.

This is a perfect example of an emerging structure being introduced to me. These opportunities present themselves all the time. It is up to you to place it in your architecture and focus on developing it.

> *Note: Like that particular VP, I was highly motivated to stand out and rise above my peers. I recognized this as an opportunity to distinguish myself, so I focused on being successful with it. My desire to learn and apply the model got me noticed, and within nine months, I was promoted again. I had only spent 16 months as a front-line manager before getting the opportunity to take on a more significant role (which came with more money, visibility, and recognition).*

Layer 4: Aspirational Structures

We each have professional aspirations that we hope to achieve in our careers. These personal ambitions could either be extrinsic or intrinsic.

With most of these aspirations, you will need to change or alter how you work or how you think about your work. If you want a better work-life balance, you can either take the approach of quitting your job or stepping down to a lesser role. Or you can learn better to prioritize your time, work tasks, and relationships. There are new soft skills and structures that you will need to strengthen and create in either direction. These are your aspirational structures.

Think about where you want to be in five to ten years to identify them. If you're going to be an executive leading a large business unit, what skills are most important for that job? The ones that come to my mind are critical thinking, entrepreneurial mindset, and influence. How do those skills fit into future skill structures specific to your career ambitions?

If you want to run for public office (local, state, or federal) in your career, what skills do you need to start learning, applying, and refining now? You must begin planning and preparing for it regardless of what or where you want to be in five to ten years. Aspirational structures give you that clarity and a development roadmap.

> *Tough Talk*
> *Most people believe earning an advanced college degree (Master's or higher) is the best way to achieve extrinsic career goals. While this is an avenue, it has limitations. Most notably, it fails to address the skills most important to your career. If advanced degrees were the best approach, a Ph.D. (or equivalent) would be a prerequisite to being an executive at mid to large companies. The brutal truth is that it's not a prerequisite.*

In Chapter 22, you will be introduced to the steps needed to create your architecture. Your goal until then should be to learn the 12 skills that make up the CYA and begin building your skills structures.

Knowledge Check
Section 2

Grab a pen and paper and answer the questions below to check your new knowledge from Section 2:

1. What are the three parts of the recommended learning approach?
2. At which part do most individuals stop (thus failing to maximize their learning)?
3. Linking occurs when you apply more than one domain or soft skill to progress a _____ or an _____ towards a conclusion.
4. What are the three ways you can start to link skills?
5. A cognitive trigger is that _____ which speaks up or that _____ feeling you can't shake when you feel something more is needed.
6. What are the two best tools you can use to improve your skills?
7. A skill structure is the _____ of soft skills that are _____ of a more _____.
8. What are the four layers that makeup skill architecture?
9. Personal architecture is a complex, carefully designed set of skill structures that are both _____ and _____.
10. True or False: The more consistent you are across the three domains when performing your newly acquired skills, the greater your likelihood of rising above and standing out among peers.

(1) Learn, Apply, Refine (2) Part 2, Apply (3) thought, activity (4) Recognize cognitive triggers, Utilize both a daily journal and a plan on a page, Focus your efforts on performance magnifying skills (5) voice, gut (6) a daily journal and creating a daily plan (7) arrangement, part, complex construct (8) Primary, Developing, Emerging, and Aspirational (9) Static and Dynamic (10) True

Section 3 - The How You Think Domain

At the end of this section, you will:

- Have learned about the four breakthrough skills that make up the How You Think domain.
- Complete several applicable lessons that you can start using today to demonstrate each skill and begin to make progress in your personal development.
- Understand what makes this domain so crucial to your long-term success.

Image 15: The How You Think Domain

Most popular literature and models on soft skills development have to do with this mindset, making my research into it the most complex of the three domains. This was because conventional thought would suggest that all 12 of the breakthrough skills which make up the architecture could, in theory, be part of the how you think domain. But, as you will learn, that is not the case.

Quick Facts & Findings of Research Study

- The four breakthrough skills that make up the how you think domain are; critical thinking, emotional intelligence, execution, and entrepreneurial mindsets.
- The How You Think domain is frequently the starting point to create skill links through the other two domains.
- Most leadership or people development training focuses the majority of their time on emotional intelligence but fails to address the root skills needed for you to be successful.
- Two of the top 5 most sought-after soft skills are part of this domain (critical thinking and emotional intelligence).

Chapter 10
Critical Thinking

DURING CONVERSATIONS WITH MANAGERS, human resource professionals, and executives, critical thinking is often the first skill they bring up, and it tends to monopolize quite a bit of the discussion.

Regardless of industry, size, or financial performance, every organization actively seeks job candidates and employees with critical thinking skills. The attributes they use to describe individuals with this skill set are; problem solvers, strategically minded, able to plan and work steps ahead, and data-driven. The skills associated with critical thinking are difficult to teach through on-the-job training. As a result, most organizations have to inject it through hiring practices instead of trying to elevate within their existing workforce.

Your options to learn critical thinking are usually confined to traditional education platforms, such as colleges and universities, or by obtaining expensive professional certifications. In a 2019 survey of more than 400 graduate students, critical thinking was ranked highest of the 12 break-through skills that students indicated that they expect to learn while attending graduate school. Historically speaking, this skill is the one we associate most with a person's intelligence, business savvy, and ability to think strategically.

But this isn't really what critical thinking is.

Critical thinking is how an individual analyzes, evaluates, synthesizes, and applies information or observations to make a recommendation, a decision, or action (see Image 15). That might have been a bit much to take in. Let me simplify what critical thinking is in the real world, but first, let me debunk what critical thinking isn't.

First, critical thinking is not problem-solving. Not every critical thinking exercise is to solve a problem.

Nor is it strategic or always related to strategy work. The terms strategic or strategy are overused, poorly defined buzz words that have been accepted as the pinnacle of thought in society. Don't get consumed by believing that you must be strategically minded or develop that skill structure first because that's the popular term.

Focus on the keyword in the definition of critical thinking. It was "how."

Critical thinking is "HOW" you go about or the process you take to analyze, evaluate, synthesize, and apply information or observations.

> *Tough Talk*
> *An executive or business leader can make a decision and call it strategic*
> *without applying critical thinking skills to analyze data or evaluate options.*

Image 16: Critical Thinking Process

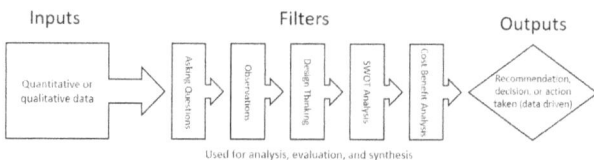

Note: the filters shown are examples of a near unlimited amount of available filters.

To become a critical thinker, you must learn how and when to leverage further analysis, evaluation, and observation instruments to form an educated opinion or conclusion to make a recommendation, make a decision, or take action based on data and nothing else. Then you will need to learn how to scale your critical thinking skills to match the demands of any given situation.

Warning
Most people who struggle with critical thinking as a skill are too consumed with getting to the output. The process is crucial for learning, applying, and refining. Once you have developed self-efficacy in the process, you can begin to expand the number of filters you have in your toolbox and fit it across more complex situations.

Inputs

Inputs can be quantitative or qualitative data that are readily available or need to be collected through surveys, interviews, observations, or reviewing the literature. While inputs for critical thinking can be substantial data sets, they can also be as simple as asking a series of questions that seek clarification, understanding, and information. Not every critical thinking situation needs a spreadsheet, a survey, or lots of data. Many will only require you to ask questions or seek out information that might not be readily available to you before making a decision, a recommendation, or taking action.

Filters

Filters are the core of what critical thinking is. What form of analysis, evaluation, or synthesis do you apply? What questions do you ask? Your decisions on selecting and using different filters will impact how you interpret the chosen inputs. To become a critical thinker, you must learn how and when to leverage other analysis, evaluation, and observation instruments to form an educated opinion, or conclusion, to make a recommendation, decision, or take action based on data and nothing else. How long you spend in this process stage will largely depend on the scale, importance, and magnitude of a particular critical thinking exercise.

No Brainer
Many different filters can be applied to critical thinking. The process can include a single filter, or in some scenarios, you might have many filters that need to be used to achieve the necessary output.

Outputs

The last element of critical thinking is the output. Commonly in the form of a conclusion drawn from the filtered inputs, it makes a recommendation, decision, or call to action.

Critical thinking as an applicable skill should always lead to an output. Collecting data and putting it through filters is a waste of time if you do not use what you have learned to make an informed recommendation, decision, or call to action.

Lesson 1 - How to quickly apply critical thinking at work

Perhaps one of the most considerable hesitations to applying critical thinking in the workplace is not having self-efficacy (see Chapter 17). As mentioned earlier, critical thinking is not just about solving problems or becoming a brilliant strategic thinker. It is the thought process of taking information, deciphering it, and coming to a conclusion. For example, you are using basic critical thinking skills at this very moment by absorbing new information, processing it, and ultimately deciding if you are going to act.

So, in theory, you are constantly applying critical thinking at every moment of the day. You apply it as you read emails, sit in meetings listening to presentations, or have a simple one-on-one discussion with a coworker. However, that is not a form or use of critical thinking that will help you rise above and stand out.

To do this, you need to learn how to apply critical thinking to your everyday work and how to use it to improve your performance. This latter part is what your boss and your employer want from you. They want (really need) employees to be strong critical thinkers capable of improving the results of their actions and activities, therefore improving the overall performance of the organization.

The great news is that there are several ways that you can quickly start to apply your newly learned critical thinking skills and have a positive impact at work. Here are the three top ways you can start today:

Approach obstacles with consistency and in a systematic way

Applying critical thinking when approaching an obstacle in the workplace gives you a systematic approach to overcoming what's in front of you. The above process moves you from sourcing data to arriving at an output that can be easily scaled to match the situation. You can consistently apply it if you see an opportunity for improvement, working on resolving a challenge, or taking on a problem. The consistency in your approach is a strength that is highly sought after. It shows that you are thoughtful, predictable, and trustworthy. Leaders value these characteristics.

> *Tough Talk*
> *Nothing frustrates me more than hearing someone say, "There are no prob-*
> *lems, only opportunities." It is so frustrating that on at least three occasions,*
> *I had suggested to the person saying it that it was time for them to join us in*
> *reality and get out of the 1990s when that useless phrase originated.*
> *Here is my rationale…*
> *How do you assess scale, impact, and priority if everything is an opportunity?*
> *You can't. If you use this language, it's time to forget it and join us in the*
> *21st Century.*

Table 2: How to differentiate between opportunities and problems

Term	Applicable workplace definition
Opportunity	An emerging circumstance that was unknown until it presented itself. Therefore, you have not made a plan or attempt towards it. Examples: (1) You recognize a breaking point in a new process, (2) A new market has emerged for your products and services, (3) The first time you observe a co-worker's feeble attempt at a new skill.
Challenge	A known breakdown, risk, or hurdle that has negative impacts on the results of activities or the individuals performing them. An attempt has been made to resolve or improve but has not yielded satisfactory advancements. Examples: (1) Your team isn't making progress on learning a new piece of software despite having completed training, and your ongoing coaching, (2) Collaboration between departments continues to be siloed after resources have been realigned, (3) a persistent hurdle continues to negatively impact you although you have taken action on it.
Problem	This well-known obstruction is detrimental to sustained individual and business performance. Multiple attempts have been made to improve or eliminate it, but all have either failed or have had limited effects. The breadth of a problem usually crosses various parts in an organization's eco-system (i.e., strategy, processes, people, technology, culture, customers, competitors, etc.). Examples: (1) Employee retention has declined for some time, (2) Team culture is negative and combative across multiple managers, and (3) Internal processes make it difficult for customers to do business with your organization.

Understand the connection between outputs and results

Critical thinking as a cognitive process should lead to an output. As described earlier in the chapter, these outputs will be in one of three forms; a recommendation, a decision, or an action. As you learn, apply, and refine this valuable soft skill, connecting your outputs to results is a particular aspect to focus on.

> *No Brainer*
> *I often get asked this. Yes, deciding to take no action is output when your data synthesis concludes that this is the best course of action.*

Having a clear line of sight between the output of your critical thinking activity and its possible results will allow you to be more predictive in your efforts. It will make you more persuasive when providing your prescribed output to others.

For instance, you see a new opportunity to upgrade your store's customer service. You collect data, put it through suitable filters, and arrive at a recommended course of action. Before presenting it to your store manager, wouldn't it be great if you quantified how your recommended action would improve customer service? And what would be the results of improved customer satisfaction?

> *No Brainer*
> *If you want to get your boss' attention and demonstrate mature critical thinking skills, then fixate on your business's leading or lagging indicators to gauge success.*

- *A leading indicator is a metric used to predict future performance.*
- *A lagging indicator is a metric that is used to measure past performance.*

> *The number of sales demonstrations you do each day is a leading indicator. The revenue resulting from the demonstrations is a lagging indicator. The time you spend with your class in small groups is a leading indicator of the test results (lagging) they get on the end-of-year assessment.*

Recognize inconsistencies in reasoning, decisions, and how work is performed

Occasionally, a concept is described in a simple image that resonates with us because it brilliantly illustrates a complex topic in a manner that is easy to comprehend. The "iceberg of ignorance," popularized by Sydney Yoshida in a 1989 study is one of my favorites.

Image 17: The Iceberg of Ignorance

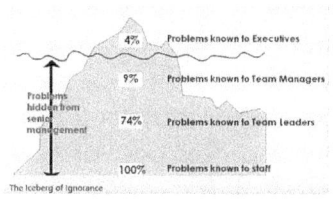

Source: Yoshida, S., (1989).
Quality improvement and TQC management at Calsonic in Japan and Overseas.

The iceberg has often been used to illustrate that the bulk of what we are looking at is hidden from sight. This outstanding example shows a limitation that executives and team managers have in knowing the problems that affect how work gets performed.

This is relevant to applying critical thinking because, unless you are at the exposed peak, there is information relating to organizational problems you can see that those above you can't. This strongly ties back to learning how to apply critical thinking on the job, with your work, and how you can improve results. Each of your known challenges and problems presents an excellent opportunity to identify inconsistencies in the reasoning and decisions made by more senior managers and how they impact how your work is performed.

This chapter will teach you the critical thinking root skills needed to collect data, put it through filters, and ultimately arrive at an output. In subsequent chapters, you will get exposed to the breakthrough skills that will help you link the proper skills necessary to turn known problems into success stories.

Lesson 2 - Understanding data and how to use it successfully

As part of developing your critical thinking skill, you will need to learn how to collect the data you need to use as input. This is not intended to be an extensive lecture on data that turns you into a data scientist or ready for your Ph.D. dissertation. But this lesson is designed to help you understand the various data types, give you an example, and start discussing what they can be used for.

This is important because each data type has a limitation and a purpose. Understanding these nuances will teach you how to leverage each type successfully as part of critical thinking. It will also help you learn which filter or analysis should be used to interpret a chosen data set. To do this, we will put a semester-long college course on data into a short lesson that covers the basics of what everyone should know.

Let's begin with where data comes from.

There are two primary sources for data and where they come from regarding your job or organization. They are internal and external. Some call these basic types little d and Big D data sets. Little d is internal data that is created from within your organization. Items such as profit and loss statements, sales trends, and employee records are all examples of internal data.

External data, or Big D, are any forms of data sourced from outside your organization. For instance, looking up a competitor on Google would be a simple example of external data. Looking at market trends in a popular trade publication or conducting a customer experience survey would all be Big D.

Depending on what you are collecting and using the data source for, you might choose one or the other source. Or you might use both.

Now that you understand that there are two sources, internal and external, you should know that there are also two main types of data, and they have subtypes.

The two main types of data are quantitative and qualitative.

Image 18: The Two Main Types of Data

Quantitative data is numerical because it uses verifiable quantities, amounts, or ranges to express values. For example, the market potential for a new product could be expressed in terms of

the size of potential dollars or the number of units sold. Your company's financial statements are a form of quantitative data.

Qualitative data, on the other hand, characterizes or approximates values. This data is typically collected through interviews, observations, surveys, or focus groups. Qualitative data can be shown or illustrated as numerical values.

An example of qualitative is when you attend a corporate all-hands meeting and catalog the types of questions during the question and answers session. You find that 40 percent of the questions asked have to do with corporate strategy, 20 percent are about people development, 20 percent of the questions asked are about a change in compensation, and the remaining 20 percent cannot be categorized. Note that your observation of questions asked was a qualitative data collection but resulted in numerical output using percentages.

Each of these two main types of data has subtypes.

Image 19: Data Subtypes and Examples

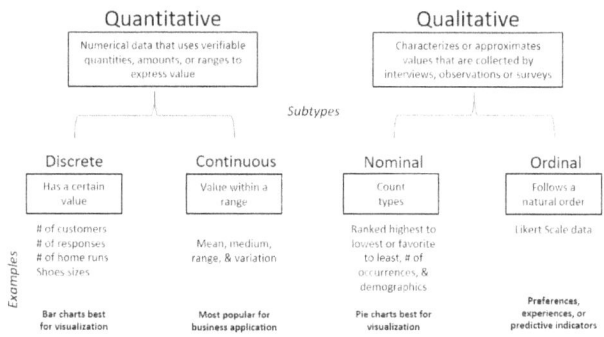

Let's first look at quantitative. The two subtypes of quantitative data are discrete and continuous data.

Discrete data is defined as having a specific value. For example, the number of employees in your company, the number of customers you have, or the number of prospective customers who respond to a marketing campaign. A popular analysis of discrete data is business process modeling. When the analysis aims to eliminate redundancies or improve productivity within a process or set of processes that make up a workflow, you can leverage discrete data to see how often and when a particular event occurs.

Continuous data is any value expressed within a ratio or interval range. This data type is the most common type used by businesses. For example, the most common types are the average dollar amount spent by a customer during a visit to a mall, the horsepower of a car, and the most popular shirt size sold in a store.

An excellent place to start is fundamental statistical analysis when analyzing continuous data. I am referring to using mean, median, range, and variation. Businesses prefer continuous data because they can use predefined values to determine how close or far away they are from targets. Business leaders can also use variances to understand why and where values are changing and trending or leverage predictive insights for planning purposes.

The two subtypes for qualitative data are nominal and ordinal.

Nominal data is qualitative data assigned a value as a number. These assigned values can be counted, but you cannot apply them to order. For example, the assigned value would not be in the natural order, but the values can be totaled to illustrate the highest, lowest, favorite, or least favorite. Nominal values are count types collected through interviews, focus groups, or observations. For example, how often did an executive mention a particular soft skill during an interview? How many times did the participants say they liked the product during a focus group introducing a new product?

A typical analysis of nominal data would include using values for grouping. The values could be grouped into themes or categories to determine the frequency or the percentage. For example, you could use nominal data to determine the demographic makeup of your customer base.

No Brainer
Nominal data is best displayed using pie charts or stacked bar graphs.

The second qualitative data subtype is ordinal data. Like nominal data, ordinal data can be assigned a value, but it follows a natural order. An excellent way to remember the difference is that ordinal sounds like "order."

The most common use of ordinal data is through a Likert scale survey. The popular 5-point Likert scale is when participants are asked to rate something by selecting Strongly agree, Agree, Neutral, Disagree, or Strongly Disagree. These items can be easily assigned a numerical value and analyzed to evaluate various areas, such as preferences and experiences, or used as predictive indicators.

Another use of ordinal data is to rank it. For example, you might want to classify customers based on their shopping preferences or experience. I always loved seeing a manager use this data type to rank employees based on the adoption of new software to promote their competitive nature to be ranked higher.

This form of gamification can positively influence employee behavior by simply applying ordinal data. Apply data when making changes at work to hold employees accountable for adoption.

Lesson 3 - How to apply critical thinking to decision-making

Decision-making is a complex and vast topic. There are college courses, numerous books, and several different philosophies relating to the art of making a decision. You will be continuously drawn back to this subject during the CYA lessons because of how crucial soft skills are in becoming a capable decision-maker.

A core characteristic of being a leader is being empowered to make decisions that affect those reporting to you or within your sphere of influence. Training on becoming a good decision-maker is often only concentrated on conceptual and procedural knowledge. Authentic learning doesn't occur until you have to make your first meaningful decision and then are required to live with the consequences.

Even in those moments, learning from the actual process and the act of decision-making might not occur. Hence, improving decision-making is a popular topic in academic and industry literature. You can become a better decision-maker through learning, applying, and refining specific knowledge like soft skills.

This brings us to this lesson. I synthesized multiple decades and genres of literature to identify the seven common decision-making practices that you should be aware of and understand the effects of each.

Tough Talk
As you review these practices, ask yourself two questions:

- *Do these practices describe the way I make decisions?*
- *And do they represent the way my organization's leaders make visible decisions?*

Self-reflection is crucial to achieving personal growth. This means that honesty with oneself is required in learning.

The first of the top seven most sought-after practices are making a rational decision, not an emotional one.

Rational decision-making indicates that it was made with evidence to support choosing between the alternatives and that some sort of process was used for evaluating that evidence. Hence, why critical thinking is an essential part of decision-making. Emotional decisions are precisely what they sound like: decisions that use your emotions as the guiding criteria.

The second practice also has to do with making a rational decision.

Is your decision being driven by data, or is it uninformed? An uninformed decision often occurs when the leader makes up their mind before receiving or collecting data. Or the leader ignores the data entirely for any number of reasons.

The key to making data-driven decisions is matching your data needs with the scope of the decision. For example, whether you should remove a step in a workflow to improve efficiency is different from deciding if you should acquire another company. You will need to learn how to scale collecting inputs and applying filters in your critical thinking process to match the scale of the decision that needs to be made.

The next practice is accountability.

This is the number one reason individuals fail to learn from previous decisions. No accountability comes from making the wrong choice. It is up to the organization, the decision maker's immediate supervisor, and even direct reports to hold that person accountable. If that person is exempt from consequences, then not only did a poor decision get made, but no learning occurred. The key to building accountability in decision-making is not the actual consequence but the process of working through why the decision was not the best alternative.

> *Warning*
> *Lack of accountability is why individuals fail to learn from previous decisions. If this is skipped and there is no consequence, the individual is free to continue making decisions in the same potentially flawed way.*

The fourth practice is speed.

Too many organizations have self-inflicted bottlenecks that prevent decisions from being made promptly. For maximum effectiveness, the decision needs to be made just in time. This phrase was coined in the manufacturing industry and meant building and delivering a product when the consumer needs it, not before or after. The most effective decision-making occurs just in time. The opposite is an individual dragging their feet in making the decision.

Top 3 Reasons why leaders drag their feet with decision-making:

- It's not a priority for them.
- Lack of self-efficacy in their decision-making ability
- Fear

Decision-making by consensus is the fifth practice.

When leaders fear the responsibility to make a decision, we often see the negative impacts of decision-making by consensus. Consensus means that everyone involved has to agree on selecting the alternative or making the decision as a group.

Your goal as a leader should be inclusive in the decision-making process, not making decisions as an agreed consensus. Inclusion in the process is when individuals who can contribute valuable data insights, experience, and judgment into the alternatives offer a position, voice support, or opposition to the options.

This is confused with an opinion and leads to downfalls associated with emotional decision-making. As a decision-maker, your aim should be to listen, hear, and consider the insights, experience, and judgment of those impacted or involved. Then it is up to you to make the best decision. Do not take a vote on it or wait until everyone agrees.

Tough Talk
Consensus decision-making is not indicative of strong leadership.

Next, the decision has to be a priority for the person making it.

Unintentional risks are introduced if the decision is unimportant to the person making it. That person might not be fully in-tune with the situation and the alternatives. Nor could they be inclined to seek additional data or decide in time.

A decision that is unimportant to a person eliminates any form of accountability. When asked to make a decision that isn't important to you and not a priority, the best choice is to push it across or down in your organization to the right person or level because it is important to that individual, which is the next practice.

This is the seventh practice in decision making is to do it at the lowest possible level in the organization.

The benefits of making decisions at the lowest level are tremendous. Increased speed due to the decision being prioritized and made improved rationally because the individual making it has increased access to the data and is closest to the work being done.

Warning
When decisions are made too high in the organization, poor practices and

risks are introduced, potentially leading to a breakdown in the entire deci-sion-making process.

As a decision-maker, it shows courage when cleanly delegating or pushing a decision that is not a priority for you to another person.

Lesson 4 – Learn how to ask questions

A characteristic associated with strong critical thinkers is the art of asking questions.

Questions are a powerful way to gather information, check for under-standing, unlock secrets, imagine possibilities, and hold others account-able. A well-placed question can alter the direction of a conversation, a venture, or a relationship. It's a skill that is undervalued by most and rarely ever taught. Yet, those who wield its power, know its influence, and recognize the need to seek to understand, then be understood are usually very strong critical thinkers. In this lesson, I examine five popular types of questions and how you can start to use each to advance your critical thinking skills.

The first type of question is the diagnostic question.

These questions are meant to identify, learn, and understand. A doctor will ask diagnostic questions to determine the symptoms of an illness so they can prescribe the correct treatment. In the same way, you can leverage diagnostic questions to understand a situation better, dive into the root causes of a problem, and learn valuable insights that would otherwise not have been known without you asking the question.

For example, if you are a people manager, you might ask a low performer on your team these diagnostic questions: What do you spend most of your time on? How do you prioritize tasks? What part of your job do you struggle the most with? What have you done in the past to try to improve?

These diagnostic questions seek to identify where the low performer has the most struggles and how you might be able to help them improve. Think about your job, your team, and your situation. What diagnostic questions could you ask to identify, learn, and understand what's going on?

Next are imaginative questions.

These questions ask people to move out of their comfort zone, think big, and reach for the stars. Imaginative questions are a great tool when problem-solving and even better when you are stuck in the conference room trying to solve a lingering problem. It's time to think big or go home.

Here are some excellent imaginative questions to get critical thinking going: What if we reframed this problem? What if we had all the money in the world? What if we could predict customer or employee behaviors? What if you could build the team of your dreams? What if we stopped and asked ourselves, what can we do differently?

Hopefully, you notice that these questions started with "What if." That is by design. If you want t people to be imaginative, you have to break through the barriers of their current reality.

The third type of question are those that help create empathy.

These questions are designed to understand others by providing them an avenue to express and share otherwise hidden feelings or thoughts. Learning empathy is the first step in building compassion, another one of the skills you will learn as part of the CYA.

Here are my favorite empathy questions: How does this situation make you feel? How is this keeping you from doing your best? What would be your ideal outcome? When are you most excited about your day? When are you least excited?

The next type of question is so often the most difficult. Those are the confrontational ones.

Confrontational questions are not meant to be aggressive or to create conflict. Instead, they are intended to hold others accountable. If you do not question the actions, motives, or ideas, you are given free rein to act or continue to act without consequence. The fault, in this case, is on you for not asking the tough questions.

Here is the best approach to asking a confrontational question:

First, state your intent for the question. These are good lines to open the conversation: I want to understand better. I want to be a better coach. I know this will be difficult, but we need to have a chat to help us.

Then, ask your confrontational question without spite, sarcasm, and judgment. Using a steady yet firm voice, ask the other person: Why did you decide on this course of action? What options did you evaluate beforehand? With what you know now, what would you have done differently? What did you expect the outcome to be?

These aforementioned were examples of good confrontational questions that were not passive-aggressive. Examples of passive-aggressive questions would be:

- What were you thinking?
- What possessed you to do that?
- Who told you that would be a good idea?
- Are you for real?

These questions risk causing the other individual to shut down or become aggressive, thus completely ruining the conversation and the intent behind your line of questioning.

The last type of question we will discuss is my favorite, the follow-up.

Good, follow-up questions move the conversation forward by continually keeping the person you are speaking with at the center of attention. The best tip for a follow-up is to ask one of the questions we just covered, listen to the response, and then take the words the other person used and ask a follow-up using their words.

You ask an employee a question to build empathy with them; "How does this situation make you feel?" He responds, "I feel like I am on a roller coaster and just hanging on for the ride."

Your follow-up questions could be "How long have you felt you were on a roller coaster?" or "What does feeling like being on a roller coaster do to you?"

You could also ask them, "What do you think we can do to help you get off that roller coaster?"

In each of these questions, you ask an essential follow-up to dig deeper into their response. This shows that you are actively listening, curious, and invested in the conversation. It also helps you be more of a critical thinker because you are diving deeper by gaining more insight and understanding of the person you are speaking with.

To become a critical thinker and show others that you are one, learn how to ask questions in everyday conversations, presentations, and important meetings. Apply these five types of questions and start to refine them to fit your personal needs.

No Brainer
A good hint is to start a journal of potential questions you could use and add to it as you grow your critical thinking skills.

Table 3: The Five Most Common Types of Questions

Question Type	Description
Diagnostic	Meant to identify, learn, and understand
Imaginative	Asks people to move out of their comfort zone, think big, and reach for the stars
Empathic	Designed to understand others by providing them an avenue to be expressive and share otherwise hidden feelings or thoughts
Confrontational	Meant to hold others accountable (not meant to be aggressive or to create conflict)
Follow-up	Moves the conversation forward by continually keeping the person you are speaking with at the center of attention

Chapter 11
Emotional Intelligence

THIS CHAPTER EXPLORES emotional intelligence (EI), its benefits, and how to develop it to better yourself and those in your circle of influence.

The commonly accepted definition of emotional intelligence is the ability to manage one's own emotions and the emotions of those around you. Empathy, self-awareness, reflection, and being well-spoken are often associated with individuals with high emotional intelligence, better known as EI.

Narrowly behind critical thinking, my research showed that employers' second most sought-after soft skill is EI. It is one of the four breakthrough skills of the Mindset in the CYA.

As I was researching this vast topic as a breakthrough skill, I wanted to understand better the root skills that make it up and present their benefits. Here are the eight benefits of emotional intelligence and an introduction to some of the root skills that you will learn in this chapter:

1. **Learn to keep your own emotions in check.** Have you ever witnessed a co-worker lose control of their emotions and have an outburst in the middle of a meeting or direct their burst towards another individual? Perhaps you know a co-worker who wears their emotions on their sleeves. Maybe you have an example of where you have let your emotions boil over and get the better of

you. Developing EI will help you better understand personal triggers and how to control your emotions so that you avoid these negatively impactful moments.

2. **Increased EI improves self-reflection.** Self-reflection is the crucial root skill of taking introspective of your actions, thoughts, feelings, and behaviors. Thinking about how you act and how you feel and doing an introspective on past or current behaviors is the best learning tool to make a change.

3. **Self-reflection is introspective of your actions, thoughts, feelings, and behaviors.** Along with improved self-reflection, learning how to have better situational awareness strengthens your emotional intelligence. Situation awareness is the art of understanding your surroundings and having the knowledge to make the most out of them.

4. **Build trust with employees, peers, and managers.** If people can predict your behaviors and know how you will respond in any number of situations, then they are more likely to trust you. Increased trust opens doors and helps solidify relationships.

5. **Managing personal stress improves your productivity, your relationships, and your health.** An essential part of EI is learning how to monitor your stress levels or being able to identify stressors that are possible triggers. By understanding your levels of stress and what causes increased stress, you can take action to reduce or even eliminate personal stress.

6. **Know when and how to ask for help.** No matter your position, role, education, or experience, we are not all-knowing and capable. Learning when and how to ask for help is crucial to having emotional intelligence.

7. **Projecting control of one's self.** This projection is part of the CYA in which you are linking two breakthrough skills, emotional intelligence, and interactions, to demonstrate you are in control of yourself. This is where most individuals break down concerning emotional intelligence. They claim or honestly believe they have emotional intelligence, but their actions, or outward projections, suggest otherwise.

8. **Better decision-making.** A root cause of why so many decisions turn sour is because the decision-maker lacks EI and makes an

emotional, not a rational, decision. To be a successful leader, you must learn to make sound, data-driven decisions without your emotions taking over.

Throughout this chapter, we will explore several root skills and describe how you can learn and start applying each to improve your emotional intelligence.

Lesson 5 - How to improve self-reflection

Self-reflection is among the most crucial root skills you can develop while working on your emotional intelligence. It is a meta-cognitive skill defined as performing inner thoughts about your actions, character, and purpose.

While this definition makes sense, the key to self-reflection isn't the actual thought that goes into evaluating your actions, character, and purpose, but rather the learnings and steps you take towards personal improvement.

> *Tough Talk*
> *Personal growth isn't achieved through self-reflection. The hard work, commitment, and consistency in action that takes place afterward allow for growth.*

Being reflective and aware of a professional development gap is only the first step in the learning process to improve or mitigate it. If you take no action toward improvement, then the act of self-reflection is a pointless endeavor.

As you learn self-reflection, it is important to distinguish between the two main types.

Reflection-on-action

This reflection period occurs sometime after the action or situation has occurred. This allows you to step away from the situation and observe it as if you were on the outside. It is a powerful way to analyze your actions, frame of mind, choice of words, overall interaction, and the outcomes or consequences.

The key to reflection-on-action is to set aside time and perform your reflection within a reasonable amount of time after the situation ends. This self-reflection period enables you to learn from your actions, evaluate their effectiveness, and take learnings from them.

With reflection-on-action, there are many tools and techniques that you can use here. A popular one usually used when teams reflect but can be applied by an individual is Wins, Learns, Changes.

Pull out a notebook and write down these three words: Wins, Learns, Changes.

How to do the Wins, Learns, Changes Exercise

1. Start by listing all the wins or what went well. If you are unsure, then it wasn't a win.
2. Next, list what you learned during the activity you are reflecting on.
3. Lastly, what would you change if you could do it over again?

This simple, rapid reflection-on-action activity is great to complete as an individual or use with your team after many important interactions.

Reflection-in-action

Note the difference between the phrase of reflection "on" and "in" action. If reflection-on-action occurs after the action or situation, then in-action means that you are reflecting while still in the act. This is very beneficial because it allows you to quickly evaluate your activities and take corrective measures, as needed, while the situation evolves.

Imagine giving a big presentation, and while you are speaking, you notice a lack of interest and participation from your audience. A person with developed self-reflective skills could quickly assess this situation and pivot during the presentation to re-engage the audience. This root skill can be used across many scenarios, both in and outside work. The key here is the quickness you go from reflection to a new course of action.

Since reflection-in-action is real-time, you need to have self and situational awareness. Consider it as thinking on your feet. Swiftly and seamlessly reflecting and making changes while in action takes experience and practice.

As a beginner, here are a few questions you could be asking yourself while doing reflection-in-action:

- Am I communicating effectively?
- Am I moving too fast?
- Am I emotionally connecting with my team or audience?
- Am I getting what I need out of this? Is the audience?
- How can I do this better right now?

Self-reflection is a critical root skill for demonstrating that you have emotional intelligence. Apply the questions above to start improving on your reflection-in-action. As you master this root skill, you will be able to reflect quicker in real-time to get the most out of your interactions.

Lesson 6 - The two aspects of improved situational awareness

We find ourselves in many different situations daily: meetings, customer visits, break room gatherings, conversations in the hallway, phone calls, emails, etc. Even in a hybrid or fully virtual work environment, we are still exposed to countless interactions with peers, customers, and managers.

Each of these presents an opportunity or potential risk to you. With each interaction, you choose if you want to make something out of it or if you will let it pass because of potential risk. Situational awareness is the most significant factor in making the most out of any interaction.

Situational awareness is having insight and understanding of your environment, the individuals in it, the space you are in, and the interaction in real-time. By being aware of your environment and those in it, you can learn to maximize interactions to your benefit by seizing moments or avoiding pitfalls.

The two aspects of improved situational awareness are:

Preparation - Preparation for what the moment will bring and what it might turn into.

Awareness - Reading the mood of the room and understanding the clues.

The first is the preparation that you should be doing every day.

Despite having nearly endless interactions, most of us don't use them very well. To do so, start observing and listening to the co-workers and leaders you interact with frequently. Learn their habits, how they work, communicate, and make decisions. Identify what part of the day they are in the best or worst mood and how they operate in meetings during different situations. For example, do they act differently towards specific individuals? Or differently when their boss is in the room? Knowing how others regularly behave can improve your situational awareness and assist you in building situation awareness.

> *Tough Talk*
> *As I mentioned, despite endless interactions, we don't use them very well.*
> *Part of the reason is that most of us take daily interactions for granted. The*
> *other reason is that we don't know how to maximize them.*

With enhanced preparation, you will notice patterns in the people around you while you observe and evaluate everyday interactions. You will see patterns in their moods, decisions, ways of thinking, and behavior. As you take mental notes on those in your ecosystem, the next step is to start making the most out of them by taking action when opportunities present themselves.

Next is the awareness that comes from context clues in any given situation.

These context clues can be anything from verbal or non-verbal clues, a feeling of tension or excitement in the room, or any social factors that might impact the emotions of those with you. Heightened situational awareness is learning how to identify context clues and use them to your advantage.

Unfortunately, we do not always see how situational awareness can be beneficial, but I suspect we all have examples of when a lapse in it becomes disastrous.

The worst missed context clues I have ever witnessed came in 2007. Todd had been with the company for more than 20 years. He was a veteran on the team and had won the coveted President's Award for top sales professional in the nation on a couple of occasions. But despite all this, a single lapse in situational awareness cost him his job.

It was early in my career, but I remember those tense moments as if I were the center of it, not Todd. We were on the same sales team, I was the up-and-comer, and he was the proven veteran. The Vice President for our sales region was making an impromptu visit to our region and wanted our team of 14 sales professionals to gather for a quick meeting the morning of his visit. It was undoubtedly a big announcement because the VP was coming to Atlanta from Boston for just the day.

After we all were seated around the office conference table, the VP started by presenting a sales update for the company and his region. This short sales update was something we had all seen many times before on quarterly conference calls, so we all knew this wasn't why he was visiting. It lasted for about 15 minutes and concluded with him encouraging us to finish strong and "don't take our foot off the gas." Then he pivoted to why he traveled in on short notice.

He pulled up another presentation on the projector screen titled Vision 2015. The presentation was a series of major strategic announcements that included aggressive targets for 2015 and how the sales teams would be realigned in the United States. While this announcement didn't affect our direct management structure, it impacted which regional VP we reported to and how we would interact with shared corporate services (marketing, finance, and logistics).

It was about 20 minutes into this second presentation when Todd unexpectedly burst into laughter. I don't recall the specific slide or the topic that the VP was speaking about, but I remember that he wasn't sharing a joke or being humorous. The entire room turned to look at Todd, who was very indifferent about his interruption and casually offered an apology.

To this day, I am not sure if it was the outburst of laughter or Todd's apathy at that moment, but it upset the VP and set a series of events in motion.

"Did I say something funny?" asked the VP straightforwardly. Todd replied with a simple "no."

The VP was not content with his answer and continued, "Then why are you laughing?"

Now embarrassed and realizing the magnitude of the situation, Todd confessed that he was looking through his email and a friend had sent him a joke. It was the joke that was to blame for his laugh.

Not impressed, the VP stepped closer to Todd and openly humiliated him by asking, "I got on a flight this morning at 5 am to be here so I could give you this news in person. Do you have no respect for me and my time not to give me your full attention?"

Our team didn't take our foot off the gas and closed the last three weeks of the quarter strong by achieving 114% of our sales target. Todd wasn't around to see the beginning of the next quarter.

> *Warning*
> *Understanding context clues can be beneficial, but missing them can be harmful not only to that moment in time but also to your reputation and your career.*

As you identify context clues, what do you do with them? How do you evaluate them so that you learn when and when not to act? Have you ever heard the phrase "Pick your battles"? That phrase screams situational awareness. If you are prepared, in tune with those in your surroundings, and recognize an opportunity for gain, then decide if this is the right moment to go for it. If not, then bide your time and pick your battle.

Lesson 7 - Learning to control your emotions

Did you know that our emotions in the workplace can tell a story about who we are?

The narrative could be favorable if we are perceived as calm, collected, and polished. Or that narrative could be unfavorable if we are perceived as stressed, always in a frenzy, angry, or too prideful.

Your goal should be to project the image that shows you are in control of your emotions and that you are someone who can be trusted, relied on, and is a leader among peers. When learning to keep your emotions in check, a few tips and tricks will help you along the way.

It might be a sense that the hair on the back of their neck is starting to stand up or an increase in heart rate. Maybe a flurry of thoughts is going through your mind. These are all indications that something is building and might happen. As you learn to be self-reflective, you will start to recognize how and when your emotions begin to develop, which will become a trigger for you to take the appropriate action.

Here is an excellent example for us all to relate to. Have you ever received an email where you were accosted by a co-worker or, worse, a manager upset you? Their snarky comments or passive-aggressive insults send your emotions spinning. You quickly feel a burning desire to respond with the same fury and over-the-top blistering response that will surely put the affronting person in their place. Somewhere in the back of your mind, a gentle voice suggests that maybe this isn't a good idea.

There it is! Your spidey-sense. What will you do next? Do you hit send or delete? This could be an indicator of your emotional intelligence maturity.

No Brainer
To keep your emotions in check, start recognizing when your emotions begin to build, or what, or who sets you off. This will help you decide the appropriate course of action.

In the early scenes of the award-winning Broadway musical *Hamilton*, Aaron Burr's character gives some advice to Alexander Hamilton: Speak less, smile more. In the scene, Hamilton has just arrived at Princeton College and seeks out Burr. When he finally meets him, Hamilton's character is consumed with emotions and spills his every thought, dream, and intention at that very moment. Burr is taken aback by the conversation and provides Hamilton with advice.

I give you the same advice today: Speak less, smile more. In a world where words matter and when emotions can overtake you, you are demonstrating control over your emotions and keeping them in check by saying less. Don't use eight words when four will do. Don't jump on a soapbox and ramble on. Here are my top tips:

Tip 1: Recognize the building of personal emotions and take the right action.

Think before you speak or respond to a question. If you are in the middle of a run-on sentence and recognize it, close the sentence and move on. As for smiling more, remember that people who smile often are considered more approachable and generally happier.

> *No Brainer*
> *Speaking less and smiling more is a classic win-win.*

To successfully control your emotions, you will need to keep the tone you use when speaking to a measured, calm projection of words. We are not suggesting that you talk in a monotone for every situation. There are certainly times to show excitement, frustration, and discontentment. But overplaying these tones waters down their effect and builds the perception that you only have one emotion. Neither creates the reputation that you want long-term.

As with tone, body language tells an emotional story you must be aware of and in control of. Do you sit back with arms crossed in meetings, with a scowl on your face? Do you fidget on your phone? Or do you lean into the table with your pen, ready to take notes? Each indicates your level of engagement, and an astute observer can judge your emotions at that particular time. When in a heated or intense conversation, do you throw your hands around to make your point?

While your words may be measured and your tone in check, overly aggressive body language can show a lack of control over your emotions.

Tip 2: Tone matters just as much as your words.

Are you like me in that you have a generally negative slanted mindset? In other words, is your glass half empty all the time? Or are you blessed with the social benefit of being optimistic, genuinely happy, and pleasant as your default state of mind? We all have a steadfast, go-to mindset that is our everyday emotional state.

Our thoughts, behaviors, and responses feed off this state of emotion, which can be helpful or harmful to our outward projections of emotional control.

Tip 3: Identify your emotional patterns and starting point.

Years ago, I had a co-worker who had a poor, pitiful me mindset. He blamed others for his shortcomings and lack of opportunity and would not take self-responsibility. This mindset was the starting point for his emotions, and with a lack of emotional intelligence, most of his interactions and thoughts originated in a place of negativity and contempt.

Over time, as a co-worker, his attitude waned on peers, and we each started to avoid conversations with him. Despite many experiences and strong critical thinking skills, his ideas were quickly rejected or ignored. This example might seem extreme, but it's not.

> *Warning*
> *We all have emotional patterns, and for some of us, our usual mindset slants towards negativity. If this is you, you must take action to find optimism. Start by changing daily habits, especially morning habits. Lesson 35 in the Influence section offers good tips on eliminating negative influences in your workplace.*

As with learning all soft skills, you have to commit to learning how to control your own emotions. How do others perceive you? Are you calm, collected, and polished? Or stressed, always in a frenzy, angry, or too prideful? If you are closer to the latter, what will you do about it? What level of emotional intelligence will you show?

Lesson 8 - How to successfully ask for help

Recognizing and having the courage to seek help shows mature emotional intelligence. It signals to others that you are humble, looking to learn, and willing to be vulnerable by asking for help. More importantly to many of us who want to advance in our careers, hiring managers want to know that you are self-aware, coachable, and willing to learn. You can show all three of these root skills by simply asking for help when it is needed.

The personal qualities of an individual with the courage and humility to seek help are widely admired.

Knowing when to ask for help means that you should understand how to recognize the signs that you need help. Here are three everyday work-related situations where you should realize you could benefit from learning and need to send up a flare.

Situation 1: When you start a new task or project that you have never done before.

You have been gifted with this opportunity to learn something new and grow professionally by taking on new tasks. The manager who assigned it to you wants to see you jump in feet first and learn from the experience. But, there is a small catch: you might not know how to start or complete the new work. And that is not only okay, but it's expected.

Part of emotional growth is learning that you will need to ask for help from time to time, and that's a sign of strength, not a weakness. Maybe it is the help you need in getting started with the new task by finding out where to find information or whom to speak to. Or simply asking what has worked or not worked in the past when others performed the work. When starting a new task or project, you should seek early assistance, especially if it is a high-visibility project or a task with increased risk.

Situation 2: You don't have a clear vision of what success should look like or how to achieve it.

If you start or perform a task and don't know what defines success, you need to ask for clarity. You could quickly be going down the wrong path and risk losing all your hard work. Or worse, get it wrong and have to face negative consequences. Ask for help to define what success looks like and what realistic goals you should set. This is important because you never want to over-promise and under-deliver. Don't be stubborn and not ask for help. If you don't have a clear answer and a clear line of sight to what success looks like and how you can achieve it, ask for help.

> No Brainer
> *Starting a stretch assignment is a great time to ask for help. It shows humility and will ensure you get off on the right foot.*

Research has shown that a typical breakdown in the workplace has unclear goals. You need to ask if you don't understand or know what success looks like or your goals. Show courage in asking for clarification.

Situation 3: You get stuck or know you are not progressing towards your goal.

This seems like an apparent time to ask for help, but very few people do. Fear is the most common reason individuals don't ask when they know they should.

Fear of rejection, looking weak or incompetent, and losing status. This is where humility and self-awareness collide with another CYA skill, courage. If you are stuck or struggling to advance towards your goals, dare to ask for help. What should you be more fearful of, recognizing that you need help and asking for it or continuing down the path you are on and getting it wrong altogether?

Failing is a crucial part of personal growth. As you progress in your career, there will be tasks, projects, and work that you will need help with. Ask for it! Don't be a prideful fool. Make sure to check out the lesson on the 5 Ways to Fail.

You are now convinced of the need to ask for help; there are good ways to do this, like most. I have learned that asking for help isn't as simple as walking into your boss's office and throwing your hands up while decisively stating that you are stuck and need help. Well, it could be that easy.

But, I would recommend taking a different approach using these tips below.

First, asking for help requires you to link skills.

Asking for help requires the linking of a couple of different breakthrough skills. The first is the emotional intelligence to recognize that you need help. Second is the courage to ask or seek it out. Next is the resourceful-ness in knowing whom to ask for help. Once you schedule a meeting or a call, you interact with the person, and you will need to show daring candor in being honest where you need support. Lastly, have an execution mindset to follow through on the suggested help. Here is what that skill link would look like:

Image 20: Common skill link required to ask for help

Once you have linked these skills and made the approach to ask for help, three elements you have prepared for that conversation.

Have proof of what you have tried (or are considering).

Make sure you have proof of what you have tried or started to evaluate alternatives or options. If you are going to a peer or your boss, they surely would want to know what you have tried thus far or what you have considered. Your goal in asking for help is for them to evaluate your crit-ical thinking process and have them understand your approach as you see it. Then, give you advice and coaching on where and what you should do.

If you have not started the new task or project, make sure you compile alternative courses of action and weigh the risks and benefits of your different options.

- Give them a well-thought-out plan to react to
- Show proof of what you have tried and why it's not working
- Show you have tried

- Link your Courage skills and give them the facts, the truth; don't ignore anything.
- Show Daring Candor

Create a plan or course of action.

The next tip is to create a proposed plan or course of action to help you achieve your stated objectives. Give the person whom you are asking for help a well-thought-out plan as something to react to. Talk to them about how you see the situation and what you believe is the right course of action based on the information and data. If they are the right person to ask for help, they will weigh your proposed plan and coach you by highlighting risks and opportunities for improvement or showing you where you need corrections.

Be willing to show daring candor.

The last tip is to show daring candor. Don't sidestep the facts, don't ignore the root causes, or fear the truth. If you know where you need help, provide the specific details of why you need it and where you are hung up. Don't try to sugarcoat or downplay it.

If you do this, you might not get the help you require and might have to return later for additional support. You will often be further lost or off course by having to return for help because you sidestepped or failed to have candor. You must avoid this situation by showing candor the first time you ask for help.

To be successful in asking for help, make sure to use all four of the elements we just discussed. Prepare to link skills, show proof of what you have tried, bring a proposed action plan, and show daring candor by not sidestepping challenges or root causes!

No Brainer
Daring candor is being open and honest in expressing your informed point of view no matter who the audience is.

Chapter 12
The Entrepreneurial Mindset

MOST OF US associate the word entrepreneur with someone who takes on personal and financial risks to start a business. That is entirely correct. However, I am going to alter that definition a little.

The definition I use for an entrepreneur includes any person who takes calculated risks to change or improve a situation. These individuals assume risks, take the initial steps, and play an essential role in creating a plan and execution. The necessary mindset to start a successful business is very similar to the mindset a person needs to have if they want to be an agent of change in their organization.

For example, if you are a new department leader and you see a need to change the culture of your department, you will need to invest energy, resources, and time to improve the culture. This inherently takes on risks. The mindset you must have is the same as an entrepreneur starting a new business. I dove deep into my experiences and research literature to understand the entrepreneurial mindset and the traits you will need to develop.

Here is a quick introduction to the six traits that make up the entrepreneurial mindset:

Trait 1: Takes the initiative

When they see an opportunity, they take it. They don't ask permission or wait for others to act first. They know that taking action is the essential trait of any entrepreneur.

> *No Brainer*
> *Individuals with an entrepreneurial mindset are not couch potatoes or followers.*

Trait 2: Knows how to ideate

To develop a strong entrepreneurial mindset, you must learn how to ideate and brainstorm where all possibilities are on the table. Not all great solutions for a business start-up or how to solve a persistent work problem are big-bang ideas. The entrepreneurial mindset acts as an incubator that allows ideas to flow openly and be greeted with enthusiasm.

Trait 3: Prototypes and experiments

You know how to take the initiative and ideate, and now you have an idea or potential solution. It's time to prototype your concept and experiment to see if it is viable. Most individuals bypass prototyping their ideas and move to pitch them to their organizational leaders. I don't suggest skipping this. Test, refine, and improve your concept through prototyping so that any potential flaws have been worked out when you do a pitch or create it.

Trait 4: Knows how to fail

Taking on calculated risks as an entrepreneur will not always go as planned. Being able to fail, learn, and apply those learning is the most excellent separator between those who can succeed and those who are pretenders.

Trait 5: Knows how to pitch an idea

Ideas and solutions have to come to life for them to become great. It takes passion, persistence, and an engaging story of the possibility to move others to action with you. Imagine if Steve Jobs failed to successfully pitch the idea of digitizing music to production companies and recording artists. If he has not been able to pitch this brilliant idea, we might all still have killer CD collections.

Trait 6: Debunked the magic bullet

The magic bullet theory suggests that your first idea will be the best, which is the one you should risk it all with. Magic bullets don't exist. You have to develop the root skills that have been outlined here to develop your entrepreneurial mindset.

As you explore this chapter, you will learn how to perform many of the root skills that develop into personality traits. By learning, applying, and refining them in your professional life, you will be able to shift your mindset toward an entrepreneur, show a willingness to take on new challenges and risks, and go above and beyond your current stature.

Lesson 9 - How to take the initiative

In a recent study, I asked more than 100 senior managers, "What behaviors did they want most from their employees?" Among the top, three most mentioned behaviors were taking the initiative.

One senior Vice President described the lack of initiative from his company's 80,000 employees as the "kryptonite that was preventing them from being super."

One Fortune 100 Human Resources executive observed that her global senior management team was made up of individuals who took the initiative and were proactive in their careers. It was that behavior that helped them get to where they are now. But, then she noted that "those sought-after behaviors are no longer present" on her team.

Top 5 most mentioned behaviors from a 2021 study that included 104 senior managers:

- Focus on adding customer value
- Prioritize your work
- Take more initiative
- Be more resourceful
- Show integrity in all that you do

Regardless of your role or position in your organization, being proactive and taking the initiative before being asked is a sought-after and highly rewarded root skill.

For instance, imagine seeing an opportunity at work, proactively jumping in with your critical thinking skills, and starting to figure out a possible solution. During your next team meeting, your boss brings this situation up. After a few seconds of no one answering, you say that you have recognized the opportunity, started to research it, and have begun a plan. How would your manager receive that? In my experience, it would not only be received well but that behavior would be celebrated.

But, take that example a step further.

What if you recognized an opportunity and went directly to your boss with a strategy, a resource plan, and a simple cost-benefit analysis illustrating it was a worthy investment for the team? There is no need to wait for a team meeting and your manager to bring it up. You saw something, a need, a challenge, an unrealized prospect, and you were proactive by taking action.

> "Real change in society must start from individual initiative." - Dalai Lama

This is the core of what makes up the entrepreneurial mindset.

Recognizing an opportunity or a problem and taking the critical first step is a highly sought-after behavior. The most important lesson to take away from this lesson is that it is not the recognition of a problem or opportunity. It is the critical first step of taking action and being willing to learn as you go.

That last part, "learns as you go," is vital to career development. To take the initiative, often, you will have to act without knowing what you are doing. You must be willing to act with the knowledge that you will learn as you go, and you will be able to execute at a high level after a short learning curve.

Here are a few ways to be more proactive and show more initiative in your daily job.

The first way might shock you, but it needs to be reinforced. Do your job!

Turn your everyday job requirements in on time. If you have a weekly time card due, turn it in on time. If your expenses or other report are scheduled on a particular day each month, ensure they are turned in on time. These types of repetitive daily or monthly tasks are commonly called professional hygiene. If you have poor professional hygiene, it gives the impression that you are unreliable, nowhere close to being a proactive employee, and have no desire to take the initiative. You don't want that negative perception.

> *Tough Talk*
> *Taking the initiative doesn't start until you have shown that you can perform everyday tasks.*

The second way to take the initiative is to start small and build a good reputation for being a go-getter.

Look for opportunities to volunteer or be a part of teams collaborating on a project or towards a goal. This will show that you are interested in the work you are doing and that you want to contribute to the overall success of your team and company.

Next, it's time to go above and beyond.

Ask your boss, "what can I take off your plate?"

Most likely, your boss will have no idea how to respond to your question. So, when you get a weird look from them or your question is followed by an awkward silence, make sure you follow up by saying that you know they have some simple tasks that take up a lot of their time and that you would like to learn and take them over so that they can focus on more critical activities.

Examples of these are: if your boss has to submit a weekly sales report, perform inventory, or attend a status meeting. These are all great activities that you can volunteer to learn how to complete and show initiative.

The last way to show more initiative at work is to listen for opportunities where others have not volunteered or have been unable to be successful in improving or completing.

This always happens, and this chance shows that you are being proactive.

Years ago, I had a manager who would ask for volunteers to perform a monthly, repetitive task. After a couple of months of hearing her request, I told my boss she could stop asking for volunteers and that I would take this task on as part of my everyday duties. She was extremely grateful, and within a small amount of time, she presented me with more opportunities to learn and take on more critical tasks.

My influence on the team started to grow, and I quickly got noticed not only as a good performer but as a high-potential team member. Taking an activity off my boss's plate contributed to opening so many other doors for me. Over the next eight years with that company, I rose from a sales team member taking the initiative to a Director leading a $60 million sales division with more than 50 employees under me.

Taking the initiative to solve a problem or taking advantage of an opportunity that no one else is working towards can go a very long way in helping you advance in your career. It is also a great way to expand your knowledge and influence.

Lesson 10 - Learning how to create big ideas (that work!)

> "I begin with an idea, and then, it becomes something else."
> Master artist Pablo Picasso

Like with all Masters, the creative process requires preparation, practice, and an entrepreneurial mindset to unleash the raw possibilities of big ideas.

Not all of us, myself included, are overly creative. Yet, we all possess basic imaginative skills to be. We just need to learn how to unleash it.

Let me introduce the art of ideation. The most enjoyable aspect of the entrepreneurial mindset is crafting ideas and solutions to solve a persisting problem, need, or emerging opportunity. Some refer to this process as brainstorming, but that is only a tiny part of the greater ideation process.

Ideation is the creative process of developing, refining, and communicating ideas.

While not a new concept, it has only recently achieved widespread popularity, thanks in part to the expansion and influence of the tech industry and the growth of design thinking. Ideation is the third phase in the traditional design thinking process. The most important takeaway from the definition is that it is a creative process. An individual or team can apply it within an organization to break norms, think outside the box, and rapidly generate ideas that would otherwise not come to light.

First, as individuals, we can quickly discover thoughts in rapid progression where no idea is too big, too small, too off the wall, or not good enough. This exercise breaks the boundaries that usually confine us to a way of thinking or how we view a defined situation. Ideation broadens our capacity to solve through a predefined creative process that steps us through exercises designed to promote cognitive improvement.

Have you ever heard that two heads are better than one? Or four heads better than two? If so, you will quickly understand the creative power that can be leveraged when a group or a team comes together to ideate. Diversity of thought and experiences brought together by a team magnifies the output through unveiling radical possibilities.

No Brainer
The key to ideating as a team is to create a safe environment where titles are left in the hallway outside the room, and all ideas are celebrated as possibilities. Without equality, the creative energy might evaporate, and the effort will be wasted.

The creative process that is ideation is not without its critics. It is not unusual for executives and managers to not see the inherent benefits of the diversity of thought and rapid idea creation through a defined process.

The most common objection is the fear that the effort will take too long and not result in a viable solution. In other words, the risk outweighs the benefits. This can be the case if the creative process is rushed, not given the proper procedural justice, or equality is not established in the proceedings.

Warning
All stakeholders must be supportive and buy into the ideation process. If they do not, any idea or solution presented and prioritized from the effort might be met with skepticism.

A trick to help create buy-in at an executive or senior manager level is to include influential leaders in the team of individuals doing the ideation. Set the stage for equality in the work and have a dedicated facilitator capable of maintaining forward progress and creative energy.

Here are six best practices to improve rapid ideation and yield outside-the-box solutions (hint: these can also be applied if you are working virtually):

I suggest a minimum of 30 minutes of creative brainstorming. If you are in a larger group, break everyone into teams of 4 to 6. Don't hesitate to extend the time if you see a lot of energy and engagement in the room.

1. **Time-box your exercise.** Don't let this become a drawn-out process where distraction can creep in.

2. **Get up out of your seat!** Getting up and moving around to form small groups will make for a more inviting atmosphere and help get the blood flowing. Sitting at a desk, table, or conference room is not ideal for creative thought. Use a collaborative, online whiteboard to simulate this when working remotely. See my note at the end of this lesson on popular choices.

3. **There are no bad ideas.** Nothing kills an individual's ideation engagement faster than being told their idea isn't good. Be receptive to all ideas and build off of each.

4. **Everyone participates.** If you see someone take a backseat, then ask them what their ideas are and encourage them to jump in.

5. **Do frequent playbacks.** After writing down your big idea, share them with others and build off the creative energy in the room. But stay focused on your prompt and don't get into the weeds or the details.

6. **Prepare before you start.** Ideation can be an impromptu exercise, but it needs to be free of distractions and in a space conducive to collaboration and thought. In other words, a common area at work or the cafeteria might not be the best space due to possible distractions. A library or other quiet place might not be ideal either. Another preparation tip is to have the right tools readily available to work with. We love sticky notes, sharpies, and easel flip charts. Whiteboards with dry-erase markers work well too. You will need the tools to rapidly write down or draw out ideas and place them where everyone can view them.

No Brainer
Once you start applying ideation to generate ideas rapidly, you will need to make small investments in supplies. The great news is that they will always be around and available to be used once you do. A LOT!

Now that you have the six best practices let's talk about the simple 4 step process for ideation.

Step 1: Use a prompt

The first step is to start with a single prompt; a needs statement, a definition, or scope of what you are ideating on. This should be written down on your easel pad or whiteboard where everyone can see it. There are three benefits to writing the ideation prompt or scope down:

- The first benefit is that you have provided boundaries for what you are the solution for. This written prompt will help keep people focused and find solutions to what is in front of them.
- The next benefit is that we need to visualize the prompt to comprehend it. This will improve the creative process and the team's engagement. It's no fun when you don't write the prompt down, and you have to be constantly repeating it.
- The third benefit of writing down the prompt is recording and documenting the exercise. Make sure to take many pictures of the output showing the written prompt and all the great ideas. This will help everyone remember what was discussed during ideation.

Step 2: Get writing (or sketching)

The fun part is step two, which is to start generating ideas. Make sure to write before you speak so you capture your thoughts. A good tip is to think of your idea as a storyboard and sketch it out. Visually drawing it out is more inspiring and helps tell your story than just writing a few words.

As you generate thoughts, make sure you listen to what others say about their ideas. This will spark new ideas or help refine those of others. After an idea is written down, or drawn, post it on the whiteboard or easel pad under the written prompt.

No Brainer
Remember that this part of the activity should be time-boxed.

Step 3: Make time to hear from each other

The third step in the ideation process is to conduct a playback where a couple of selected team members review all the captured ideas. This allows for further discussion and maybe even new ideas to be created. It is also important to start to put themes, like-minded, or similar ideas together. By theme, you will begin to show a pattern of possible solutions, which will help in the last step, prioritization.

Step 4: Prioritize the ideas

You and your team have ideated possible solutions using a written prompt. But the work isn't done. You now need to prioritize the solutions as the last step before planning your work.

There are several ways to do this.

Democratic voting is often the best and quickest way to determine which ideas should be a priority. I use the simple method of providing each team member with three little stickers and asking them to put their three stickers on their favorite ideas. They can put a single sticker on three different ideas or use all three of their stickers on a single idea.

The bottom line is that each person has three votes to distribute any way they wish. After a few minutes of voting, count the ballots, and rank them from the highest to lowest vote-getters. Now you have prioritized your big ideas and have completed the ideation process.

As you have learned this process for ideation, you can deploy it for both small and tremendous opportunities, with small teams, large workshops, or as an individual. But, follow the tips and process outlines to achieve maximum value.

> Note: if you work remotely, you can still ideate and apply the six best prac
> tices listed above in this environment. There are several collaborative tools
> and whiteboards that can assist you when working remotely. My preference is
> Mural. But Miro and Bluescape are also very popular. Here are their websites:

- *mural.com*

- *miro.com*
- *bluescape.com*

Lesson 11 - Making the most out of prototyping & experimenting

Now that you have ideated to create potential solutions and have prioritized them, it is time to test your solutions. Prototyping and experimenting is often a process that is rushed through, watered down, or skipped altogether. As an individual developing their entrepreneurial mindset, you must learn and clearly understand the importance of testing an idea or solution before scaling it. Let's first start with a definition for each.

Prototyping is the process of developing a model, a sample, or a minor release of a product or solution you want to test.

For example, if you are developing a new piece of software to manage inventory, you would want to do a minor release with a subset of your stock to test the software's functionality and ability to meet your needs before a full-scale launch. Product development is an excellent example of how prototyping is used to great success.

For example, Tesla developed several full-scale prototypes of its Cybertruck to perform many tests. Before showing it to the public and committing it to production, this was all done.

In our context, experimenting is a fancy word for testing a prototype or a solution with your targeted audience, users, or consumers. It is simply defined as trying out a new concept or design.

Experimenting can take many forms, and multiple experiments can be done when testing a prototype.

Take the Tesla Cybertruck example. The new truck design and prototype had to undergo several performance, safety, and capability tests to ensure it performed as designed. But, it also had to be evaluated from a consumer market perspective. Tesla had to determine if its design appealed to consumers and how it was rated versus other competitive trucks in the market. The company then had to determine what the market would pay to own one. These are examples of experiments that could be done to test the feasibility of a solution and prototype.

Unfortunately, a lot of time, prototyping and experimenting get skipped. It is safe to say that Tesla would not skip these steps before the mass production of a new truck. But would you skip prototyping and experimenting if you implemented a solution to reduce manufacturing defects? Or streamlining your company's decision-making process by eliminating layers of historical bureaucracy?

Neither of these examples provides a clear-cut answer to support performing or skipping prototyping and experimenting.

There are two key questions you need to ask when determining whether or not to prototype and experiment:

What are the risks if I do not create a prototype and experiment?

And, what happens if I choose not to create a prototype and experiment, and I get it wrong?

For the first question on the risk of not creating a prototype and experimenting with it, you should consider all potential risks, such as financial, employee morale and attrition, loss of productivity, opportunity costs, etc. If you deem the solution low risk, move forward without prototyping and experimenting.

If you determine that your organization could have harmful effects if the solution is not tested, then take the time to do it.

The second question is designed to build dual redundancy into your decision to or not to prototype and experiment with a solution.

Sometimes we are blind to potential risks or ignore them due to various types of pressure. When you ask yourself and your team what happens if we choose not to test and get it wrong, and that answer doesn't scare you or cause you and your team to hesitate, prototyping and experimenting might not be necessary.

If by asking this question, you hesitate or it causes a moment of fear, then take the time to prototype and experiment.

No Brainer
It is better to find potential flaws during testing than after you push it out to your mass audience. This allows you to make corrections quickly without massive impacts on costs, time, or reputation.

Lesson 12 - The five ways to fail

We all experience bumps, setbacks, and detours when trying something new or taking on more significant tasks. Failure is part of the entrepreneurial process.

We must be prepared to fail, learn, and apply those learnings to move forward and achieve what we set out to. But we don't have to fail in a detrimental way to our long-term success. Learning how to fail is an integral part of the entrepreneurial mindset.

Here are the top five ways to fail:

Quickly

Don't be the frog that sits in the water and waits for it to boil. Failing quickly will highlight flaws in design, concept, or execution. Ignoring early signs leads to massive breakdowns that could ultimately be unrecoverable. The opposite way to failing quickly is slowly. Hence, the frog in water analogy.

Observe the littlest negative comments, snags, or breaks when ideating, prototyping, and experimenting. These could amount to nothing or be the beginnings of failing slowly.

The quicker you identify a failure point, the quicker you can learn and apply those learnings.

Cheaply

In 2017, I witnessed a company try to move their entire 20,000-person workforce and 80 years of data to the cloud simultaneously. When it failed, it cost millions of dollars to rectify. The cause of the failure wasn't the scope of the solution; it was in the process. If the organizational leaders had experimented with smaller groups or data repositories, they would have identified the breakpoint and failed cheaply.

> *Warning*
> *Don't run to scale a solution or resource an opportunity too quickly if you haven't failed yet. Because when the failure occurs, and it will occur, the scale will inflate the cost.*

Frequently

Fail quickly, fail cheaply, and fail often. Frequent failure when prototyping and experimenting are ideal. If you know the story of how Thomas Edison created the light bulb, then you know he claimed to have tried more than 10,000 combinations to find the perfect solution. Frequent failure lets you identify what needs to be corrected and allows you to take action.

Most people get upset when failure keeps occurring. Rejoice in these moments. Because with each failure, you move closer to a practical solution.

Elegantly

If we accept failure as part of the entrepreneurial mindset, we must accept it as part of the learning process. Failing with grace, decorum, and dignity is far more acceptable than failing with chaos and panic. This doesn't mean you shouldn't be upset about failing; you have the emotional intelligence and the entrepreneurial mindset to know that failing is an opportunity, not the end.

Safely

This is perhaps the only reason individuals don't take risks at work and in their careers. They don't have the feeling of safety in their environment. If you are a people manager, creating a culture of safety for calculated risk-takers with an entrepreneurial mindset should be a priority.

To know if you are working in a safe environment where failure is celebrated. Take a small risk by starting a conversation with your manager to pitch a new and provide a compelling story of the possible. Their response will tell you how safe of a work environment you are in for taking calculated risks and failing.

Failing is part of the learning process, but it needs to be celebrated, not feared—welcome failure as part of personal and team growth.

Chapter 13
The Execution Mindset

THIS CHAPTER FOCUSES ON EXECUTION, or simply put, getting things done.

As part of the How You Think domain, the execution mindset is the cognitive state that propels us to get started and to get things done. It is not a complicated concept, but to master this mindset, you must learn to harness your drive and desire to perform higher than before and higher than those around you.

To understand the importance of execution, I encourage you to look up quotes for it in your favorite search engine or the growing number of books on the topic. As you see the vastness of its totality, I suspect you will get a sense of how vital execution is to fulfill a vision strategy and how your ideas will not come to reality without it. This is true not only of bold visions and daring strategies but of day-to-day life.

> *No Brainer*
> *Execution, or the ability to get things done, is one of the top differentiators among co-workers, and it plays an integral part in career development.*

Think for a moment about your resume. When you summarize your accomplishments into neat bullet points on a page, you apply past tense action words to outline what you have done. The most popular terms used on a resume and looked for by recruiters are: created, managed, achieved, launched, trained, and of course, executed.

The popularity of these words in hiring and advancement indicates your ability to get things done. It is among the most critical soft skills needed for career progression.

Of the 12 breakthrough skills that make up the CYA, the execution mindset is the easiest to learn but among the hardest to master. This is because it requires more personal commitment and consistency over time. It's not a switch you can flip on; suddenly, you begin to get things done faster and perform your work at a higher level. It has to become a way of life, or how you behave and work daily.

That is why I classify the execution mindset as a soft skill. Unlike what you will find in other books and teachings, I view execution as a skill that can be learned, applied, and refined as you progress through your career. It's not something that you are born with or a simple trait that is easy to be quickly acquired through conceptual knowledge.

Your goal is to make your ability to execute part of your professional reputation. Instead, you would have your co-workers and organizational leaders perceive that you know how to get things done versus believing you struggle with this skill.

So, how do you turn a desire to get things done into action? You learn how to plan to manage your time and workload. Each of these broad categories represents root skills that make up the execution mindset and will help you improve getting things done and stand out among your peers.

In this chapter, we will explore several topics, tips, and proven ways that you can immediately start to execute at a higher level and start building a reputation as an individual who gets the job done.

Lesson 13 - Learning how to prioritize tasks

Learning to prioritize tasks is a root skill that is rarely taught yet is critical to your success.

Whenever I am speaking with employees, managers, or executives about their ability to execute, the number one reason they say they can't get more done is lack of time. This is true for almost all of us, but it's not the actual reason why we can't get more done. As I dive into the root causes, I identify two leading reasons capable individuals fail to get things done.

The first reason is that too much time is spent putting out fires or so-called emergencies versus doing productive, required work.

The second, which we will discuss in this lesson, is that we don't know how to prioritize our work effectively.

There are many tips and tricks to help you prioritize your tasks to make the most out of your day. The goal of each is to maximize your time by focusing on the most valuable tasks and of the highest importance for your success. Anyone who coaches people on time management and prioritization will suggest you have to put the most important work first and do a better job managing fire drills.

But this is poor advice because it doesn't teach you how to prioritize tasks. You need to learn the "how" to prioritize your work. So, I will give you what I have found to be the leading practices for prioritizing your work.

To start with, you need to know and apply these three practices in your everyday work:

Learn how to say "no"

Most of us are guilty of taking on too much work by saying "yes" to everyone who asks for help. Thus, we cannot get our job done with the additional work you agree to do. Even worse, you risk completing the work in a rush and not up to a level of performance you are satisfied with. By learning to say no, you will eliminate unnecessary, unimportant tasks.

Not all tasks are equally important

This might seem like a simple concept to perform, but it's mind-blowing how often I see or hear of someone working on a low-importance task while other more important tasks get set aside.

Remember the personal superpower discussed in Chapter 6?

Consistency in your efforts to prioritize and focus on important tasks will be critical to your success with this root skill. You can't prioritize tasks on a Monday morning and by Tuesday afternoon, abandon your efforts. Inconsistency will lead to failure and not help you improve your execution ability.

Now that those quick practices are out of the way, let's talk about five approaches to prioritizing tasks and achieving a higher level of execution:

1. Modernize how you use to-do lists

The first approach is an old trick that has been proven to work. Yet, research shows that less than a quarter of us do it. We are talking about making to-do lists for the tasks you are responsible for. Lists make a difference and allow us to keep track of tasks and mark them completed once done.

I recommend using a personal Kanban board to give it a modern look and feel. Kanban boards are a visual representation of work in various stages of completeness that will help you prioritize tasks and effort. Remember, we are visual beings by nature, and learning how to exploit this will improve your execution. At your desk in your office or personal work-space, you need to have a visual to-do list or board.

2. Prioritize your work using the Eisenhower matrix

Developed by President Dwight Eisenhower, this two-by-two matrix helps you determine which tasks to focus on based on their importance and urgency.

You will need to list all the tasks, activities, meetings, and outputs you are responsible for completing. Now that you have all your tasks outlined, they should be plotted according to their level of importance and urgency.

Image 21: The Eisenhower Matrix

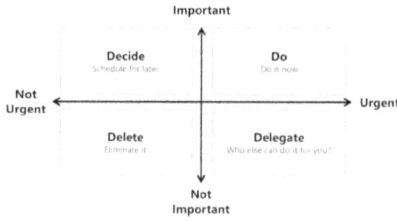

Now that all your tasks have been plotted, you need to understand each quadrant and how you should approach the tasks within it.

- Tasks that fall into the Urgent and Important quadrant should be completed as soon as possible.
- Those that are important but not urgent should be scheduled to be completed as soon as the urgent and important tasks are done.
- Urgent but unimportant tasks should be cleanly delegated to someone else.
- For tasks that are neither urgent nor important, it is recommended that you drop these from your schedule as soon as possible.

Warning
The most common error I observe when someone starts to use the Eisenhower Matrix is that they think all tasks are "important." Remember the lesson mentioned above; not all tasks are equally important. If you start plotting all your tasks and everything falls into the important category, I recommend you sit with your boss and ask them to rank order your tasks in terms of what they feel is most important for your success.

3. Be flexible and always consider the sunk cost fallacy

The sunk cost fallacy is a physiological effect when we feel compelled to continue doing something because we have already invested time and effort into it. Prioritizing tasks can be a guessing game. We might believe a task will be easy, and once we get into it find out that it requires far more effort and time than we initially thought.

That is fine, as long as you reprioritize the task given what you now know about it. When this occurs, and it will, you should re-plot it on your Eisenhower Matrix and then take the appropriate action based on its position.

> *Tough Talk*
> *Don't fall for the sunk cost fallacy. Be flexible, stop the task, and re-prioritize it with the new information on how much time and effort it requires.*

4. Work on the most important tasks when you are on your A game

Another way you can improve your execution through prioritizing tasks is to learn how to leverage the production curve.

Each of us naturally has productive peaks and valleys in our daily schedules. A peak is when we have minimal distractions and are most effective. A valley is the opposite. So, schedule your most important work during your peak times when you are most productive. That makes sense, right? Do your most important work when you are most productive. To do this, you need to figure out when you are most and least productive. Then block this time on your schedule.

For me, I am most productive after my two kids leave to go to school at 7:30 am. So, I block my calendar for the next 90 minutes to focus on getting work done because I am distraction-free, and most of our team isn't working at that time (we all work remotely, and most don't get online until 9 am).

5. Learn how to time box

If you know you work best in the morning or just after lunch. Then block that time on your calendar and eliminate the ability of others to put meetings in that time slot. Time-boxing is when you stop time on your schedule for uninterrupted work. You set a duration of time intended to get things done that are most important.

Be vigilant in this effort. If you have a time box, start and end on time and focus only on what's most important. Remember, this is your time to focus on essential tasks for your job. If a meeting is more important than your assigned work, then that meeting and its work need to be prioritized. If it's not more important, hold firm to your time box.

Each of these ways improves how you prioritize and execute proven practices. And they are infectious. Once your peers see how you can increase the amount of work you get, they will ask you how you do it. Share these lessons with them.

Warning
Lack of consistency is the number one reason most individuals fail to prioritize their work. You have to be consistent with your efforts to be successful. To rise above and stand out, you should utilize several approaches.

Lesson 14 - How to master following through on tasks

Following through means that you complete an assigned task or activity on time.

Excellent follow-through skyrockets your professional capital. The quality of work and the speed at which you complete assigned tasks positively affect your professional reputation. Leaders expect each task they assign to be completed, which is the ideal behavior for a person to have this root skill. However, multiple studies over the past decade show that most individuals don't follow through on assigned tasks or must be given various reminders to complete them. A recent Harvard Business Review (HBR) study showed that 3 out of five workers struggle with follow-through.

Even more important is that this skill transcends all careers and jobs. Imagine how you would suffer if you were a salesperson and you failed to follow through on sending over a price quote. Or if you were a teacher and had a habit of not returning calls from parents. What if you lead a team and ignore constant requests to take action on a topic you have committed to? By not having the root skill of following through, you can negatively impact the confidence of others in your ability to execute. Thus, harming your reputation and weakening your prospects for career advancement.

No Brainer
Your goal for following through on tasks is to deliver high performance at the moment it is requested or just before.

Apply these five concepts to become better at following through and improve your work execution.

1. Don't overpromise and underdeliver

When you are volunteering for a task, you need to consider two things by asking yourself:

- Do you have the availability to complete it?
- And, are you risking over-promising what you can deliver?

If you don't have time or promise too much, you will fail to deliver on the task. And this is not a situation you want to be in.

Any time you volunteer, ensure that it will be an easy win for yourself by ensuring you have the time and that it's not something you are over-promising.

2. Engage the help you need early and often

If your task requires the support of co-workers or individuals in other departments, engage them immediately. If your work depends on their ability to get stuff done for you, you need to be clear on what you need and when you will need it done. You are, essentially, giving them a deadline.

Don't hesitate to escalate this to their boss if they miss their deadline and are not responsive to your request or your actions to follow up with them. Be respectful but firm. Make sure to link your interaction and influence breakthrough skills when asking others to help.

The most important takeaway is to engage them early enough that they can plan their portion of the work.

No Brainer
It is advisable to make sure you build some buffer time for them to be late potentially.

3. We live in the 21st Century

Make technology your ally. It's frustrating to see a person get assigned a task due on a particular day, and they don't set a calendar or task reminder in their digital calendar. Or they don't leverage a personal kanban board.

Why would you not leverage the available technology for this exact purpose?

If you have completed the lesson on prioritizing your work, then make sure you add all your assigned tasks to your personal Kanban board and your Eisenhower matrix to know which tasks are most important to get done first.

Top individual task management tools:

Price as of 2022 for individual subscriptions

- Friday (Free to $4 per month)
- Google Tasks (Free)
- Asana (Free to $10.99 per month)
- Trello (Free)
- ClickUp (Free to $5 per month)
- Todoist (Free to $3 per month)
- Microsoft To-Do (Free)
- Any. do (Free to $5.99 per month, $4.49 for six months, $2.99 per 12 months)
- Sunsama ($10 per month)
- Akiflow ($15 per month)

4. Don't work in a vacuum or a silo

Set up a cadence of touchpoints with the appropriate leaders and stakeholders for larger tasks.

An update isn't required for tasks you turn around within 48 to 72 hours. If the task has a duration that could be measured in months, you need to set up a cadence of touchpoints in person or using a virtual meeting space.

No Brainer
If it's a task that will take you a week or two to accomplish, consider sending a weekly status report. My favorite status reports answer three simple questions:

- What's going well?
- What are you currently working on?
- Where do you need help?

Image 22: Example of a weekly status report

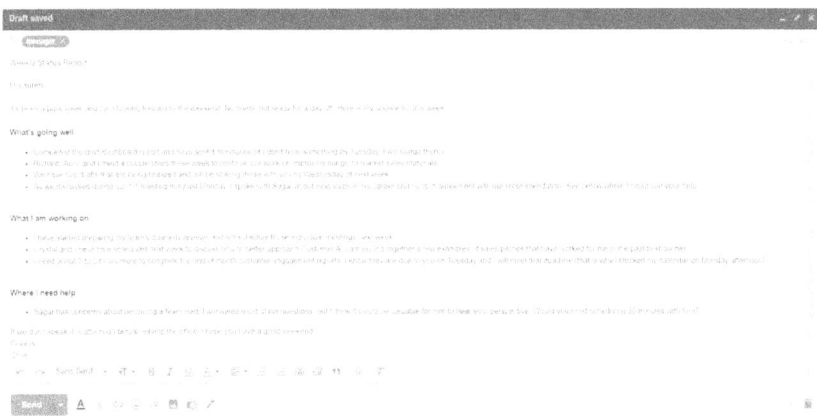

5. Understand and plan for the complete environment

The last tip to improve your follow-through is identifying potential barriers to completing any task. You should do this before you get started and have a plan to mitigate them.

For instance, if you need a particular software, request it on day one. If you need time from an organizational leader or a person in another department, then schedule it immediately. Don't let barriers prevent you from completing the task, and don't let them force you to be late or finish with work quality below what you can do.

These five concepts are easy tips to improve your follow-through. Which ones stood out to you as a way that could improve the way you execute every day?

Lesson 15 - The good ole' 30, 60, 90-day action plan

This lesson will discuss the benefits and the seven steps needed for creating a good 30, 60, and 90-day action plan. This is very important because good planning, resource allocation, and assignment of tasks are significant aspects of getting things done when working in teams.

> *No Brainer*
> *While not a new concept, the 30, 60, and 90-day action plan is the best approach to setting up an actionable work plan to prioritize tasks and execute against them.*

This classic approach allows you to break apart larger tasks using the variable of time. For example, what will you and your team get done in the next 30 days, and how do those early tasks influence what you will get done in the next 60-days? Using this planning approach, you can assign team members tasks and track them through to completion. And last, you can easily show a progression of work that has been completed and track it against your larger goal.

Here are the seven steps you need to take to set up a great action plan.

Step 1: Set up goals

As the famed author Stephen Covey suggested in his book, 7 Habits of Highly Effective People, begin with the end in mind. What is your team's goal for the completion of the plan? What are the team's goals at the end of each 30 days and then at the first 90 days? Set up goals for each 30-day increment with the understanding that the plan might extend past 90 days.

No Brainer
Write your goals down! Research has shown that you are much more likely to achieve your goals if you write them.

Step 2: Ideate and write out all the tasks that need to be completed

Make sure you and your team capture the lowest-level tasks that need to be done. If you say we need to implement new software and fail to identify all the steps, tasks, and dependencies that lead up to that, you are missing the point of creating a 30, 60, 90-day plan. When identifying all the tasks, I love using post-its and a whiteboard for this exercise. The key takeaway for this step is that all tasks need to be placed, written down, and planned out.

Step 3: Allow SME do their job

The subject matter expert (SME) or the person responsible for the task should determine the time frame to complete the task. Having the appropriate person establish the time frame creates buy-in, builds accountability for the task, and helps to set up a realistic plan. You will also need to make sure you account for and mark contingencies for individual tasks and identify those that can be worked on in parallel. Successful work plans know which charges depend on others and which can be performed simultaneously.

Step 4: Commit to the plan

After all, tasks have been assigned and placed in a time frame for completion, have everyone step back and review it for final updates before signing off. When teams are in person, have them physically sign the plan as a show of commitment. Last, make sure to distribute a copy of it to everyone.

Step 5: Set up governance

At this point, the plan has been created, and now you should establish a cadence of touchpoints to review the progression of tasks.

These meetings should be brief, and only focused on the tasks and any barriers to success. During these touchpoints, you and the team members must be open and candid when presenting your progress, the obstacles to success, and updating any changes. This is a perfect time to link your courage breakthrough skills and lead by example. When you set up touchpoints, you will also need an agreed-upon set of procedures to decide how to push tasks back to the next 30-day time frame, reassign them as needed, or escalate challenges that arise either inside or outside the team.

Step 6: Socialize the plan

Next is to share your plan with your organization's appropriate leaders and stakeholders. It is advisable to send them a status report after each central touchpoint and inform them of your progress and potential risks.

This can be done with quick face-to-face conversations, giving them access to the technology platform you are using to track the tasks, or through an email. Note that I put these three suggestions in the most to least effective order.

Step 7: Monitor progress

For creating an effective 30, 60, 90-day action plan, you must track the status and completion of each task. As your plan evolves and when your plan will be longer than 90 days, continue to add 30 days in the end. This ensures that you always have at least 90 days of actionable work planned out.

> *No Brainer*
> *This is also the time to leverage technology to track the work and set up reminders.*

Don't avoid leveraging this simple planning and execution tool for all major tasks and projects you are working on. As you apply these tips and refine them for your particular situation, you will quickly learn to manage multiple 30, 60, and 90-day plans for several workflows.

By doing this well, you will demonstrate a higher level of execution by being able to plan, prioritize, and get work done. This will allow you to stand out among peers, get noticed, and do amazing things.

> *Warning*
> *I recognize that Agile and working in sprints has become a popular way to manage larger projects. I strongly recommend Agile when you have the right skill sets and governance. But don't force an unprepared, unskilled team to work in a way they can't. This is the opposite of having an execution mindset focused on getting things done!*

Lesson 16 - How to be more productive by eliminating fire drills

Of all the lessons in this chapter, this is the area that I see individuals struggle with the most.

Urgent needs and tasks, otherwise known as fire drills at work, negatively affect your productivity and ability to execute.

Fire drills consume time, energy, and focus and prevent you from looking forward because you have to solve for the present. Learning how to decrease or stop these constant interruptions for break fixes, emergencies, or challenges will radically improve your ability to get critical work done and completely change the emphasis of your work from the present to the future.

> *No Brainer*
> *Future work can be described as strategic because you are looking forward and working towards a future goal. At the same time, urgent work is present tense.*

Regardless of its importance, no work is free from being put aside due to urgent tasks and fire drills. This was the case for The Boeing Company in 2020. On the heels of two 737-Max crashes that took the lives of 346 individuals in late 2017 and early 2018, the company was in a real crisis. Consumer confidence was at an all-time low, the stock price had dropped nearly 30%, and the resignation of their CEO Dennis Muilenburg in December 2019 made it clear that drastic action would be needed to recover.

In response, the new CEO David Calhoun and the board of directors put several vital initiatives in place to regain Boeing's prominence in the aerospace industry and put the 737-Max safely back in the sky. Among the changes announced was creating an independent safety organization that would ultimately oversee product assurance and a massive re-organization of sixty thousand engineers. But, these two fundamental changes, crucial to Boeing's future operating model, were delayed and took much longer than expected to come to fruition. The reason why?

You guessed it. Urgent work and fire drills consumed the employee teams responsible for executing these two critical board of director initiatives. When Boeing's leadership set up the teams to complete this new work, they didn't eliminate or delegate the daily job duties of the assigned team members. So, naturally, the team members were pulled back into their day-to-day tasks and spent countless hours putting out fires that were part of their regular duties. The critical work of standing up a safety department and realigning the company's entire engineering population was a secondary activity.

While this extreme example illustrates how vital work can be put aside for less important tasks due to a false sense of urgency. To decrease the number of fire drills, apply this three-phase approach: Understand, Develop, and Eliminate.

Phase 1: Understand

Fires have a cause.

A local fire marshal evaluates each structural fire to assess the damage and the root cause. Why should urgent tasks or fires at work be any different? To eliminate fire drills, the first step is to understand.

Each fire will have a root cause. Apply your critical thinking skills to identify and evaluate them. This is crucial to stopping future drills.

The next step in understanding is identifying the root cause patterns. If you are experiencing many drills, it will likely have a pattern. Here is a hint, patterns for fire drills will fall under a handful of categories. Most patterns will relate to people, processes, tools, or decision-making. Or a combination of these four categories.

No Brainer
Improved communication, clean delegation, and empowering others to be
decision-makers are the best ways to eliminate fire drills.

Another key to understanding the root cause is checking for comprehension of expectations and goals. This is often what causes the fire alarm.

Tough Talk
Research has shown that up to 40% of work-related emergencies are due to
misinterpretation or misinformation in expectations or goals. Thus, the
alarm is pulled.

Phase 2: Develop

After a solid understanding, it's time to develop a solution. Not a solution for the current fire drill, but rather solutions that will decrease future exercises.

Start with coaching on the root causes you identified in phase one. A lot of the time, you will determine that drills will be related to knowledge or the ability of others to perform their job. Think of this as teaching people how to fish, not you catching it for them.

When coaching individuals on reducing work-related emergencies, you might be coaching employees, peers, or your boss. Be ready for those potentially tough coaching conversations by linking other breakthrough skills.

Next, develop a better response or escalation plan for drills.

Of course, emergencies at work will happen, but they need to be the exception, not the norm. Create or revise your organization's escalation plans and clearly outline a RACI chart. A RACI chart identifies who is responsible and accountable, who needs to be consulted, and who needs to be informed.

When implemented and executed well, this simple tool can effectively eliminate fire drills at work.

Image 23: Sample RACI Chart

RACI Chart

	Project Manager	Strategist	Designer	Front End Developer	Back end Developer
Design sitemap	C	R	A	I	I
Design wireframes	C	A	R	I	I
Create style guide	A	C	R	C	I
Code templates	A	I	C	R	C

R = Responsible   A = Accountable   C = Consulted   I = Informed

The last step in this phase is to develop an after-action review. This allows the fire to be extinguished and you to return to the situation to reflect on the action. This reflection will make sure your fix worked and then understand better how to prevent other drills that could be similar.

Phase 3: Eliminate

To eliminate fire drills from happening, consider the following three options.

- **Make changes.** If you are a leader and the emerging pattern relates to an individual, ask yourself the hard question and determine if that person needs to be part of the team or the escalation path you created earlier. Treat patterns that illustrate breakdowns within your organization's processes, tools, and decision-making similarly.
- **Assess and possibly revamp your team's culture.** You might be part of a culture that relies on fire drills, and it might have underlying issues that need to be addressed. Part of the reason you might have so many drills is that your organization doesn't know how to fail.

- **Empower others to respond and take action in response to the drill.** Cleanly delegate the drill to another person if it isn't a high priority for your daily work. Give others the power to decide, act, and resolve the current drill. As well as future ones like it.

Learning to eliminate urgent tasks, otherwise known as fire drills, will help you to improve execution and how well you get things done.

To be successful in reducing drills, start by understanding the root causes. Then develop potential solutions to resolve what you found. Last, take bold actions to eliminate drills from happening.

Tough Talk
Reducing and eventually eliminating fire drills in the workplace is challenging. It must be a commitment that you, your team, and the organizational leader are willing to focus on and be consistent with (yep, that superpower again). If everyone is not fully committed, you will not be successful in eliminating the urgent work that is harming your productivity.

Knowledge Check
Section 3

Grab a pen and paper and answer the questions below to check your new knowledge from Section 3.

1. What four breakthrough skills make up the How You Think domain?
2. Critical thinking is _____ an individual analyzes, evaluates, synthesizes, and applies information or observations to make a recommendation, a decision, or action.
3. Which skill was ranked highest of the 12 breakthrough skills that graduate students indicated that they expected to learn when pursuing an advanced degree?
4. The two main types of data are _____ and _____.
5. Execution, or the ability to _____ _____ _____, is one of the top _____ among co-workers and it plays an integral part in career development.
6. Personal growth isn't achieved through self-reflection. It the _____, _____, and _____ in action that takes place afterwards that allows for growth.
7. What are the five ways to fail?
8. True or False: Lack of accountability is the number one reason individuals fail to learn from previous decisions.

9. True or False: The 30, 60, 90-day action plan is not a very successful way to plan and execute work.

10. What are the six traits of the entrepreneurial mindset?

(1) critical thinking, emotional intelligence, execution, and entrepreneurial mindsets (2) how (3) critical thinking (4) quantitative and qualitative (5) get things done, differentiators (6) hard work, commitment, and consistency (7) Quickly, Cheaply, Frequently, Elegantly, Safely (8) True (9) False, it is a very successful way (10) Takes the initiative, knows how to ideate, prototypes and experiments, knows how to fail, knows how to pitch an idea, has debunked the magic bullet

Section 4 - The How You Feel Domain

At the end of this section, you will:

- Have learned about the four breakthrough skills that make up the How You Feel domain.
- Complete several applicable lessons that you can start using today to demonstrate each skill and begin to make progress in your personal development.
- Understand that it's the way you "feel" that is the most significant influence on your actions.

Image 24: The How your Feel Domain

How you feel humanizes you by controlling your fear, acceptance, and perceived personal value. The four skills that comprise this domain are associated with your metaphorical heart. Mainly how you express feelings when interacting with others and demonstrate a willingness to take action; these skills are most overlooked in training and personal development because they are viewed as too touchy-feely or should already exist.

Quick Facts & Findings of Research Study

- The four breakthrough skills that make up the how you feel domain are; compassion, inclusion, courage, and self-efficacy.
- The How You Feel domain has the most significant influence on your outwardly projected behaviors.
- The courage to speak up, think outside the box and challenge the status quo has quickly become widely accepted and welcomed by most leaders
- Confidence and Self-efficacy are entirely different yet are treated as synonyms by most.
- One of the top 5 most sought-after soft skills are part of this domain (Courage).

Chapter 14
Compassion

THIS IS the introduction to compassion, a breakthrough skill in the how you feel domain.

Let's start with a simple truth that we all could agree on.

We live in a chaotic world. Political, social, and financial influences cloud good intentions and the incredible acts that many individuals exhibit daily. Social media has shrunk the world, so individual opinions and thoughts can reach vast audiences with just a few hundred characters.

Despite the attempts of a few loud voices, I believe that humanity pursues open-mindedness, acceptance, and inclusion. We all have a small part to play in the events of today. This is important because how we feel will be the path that our actions follow.

Do we just show empathy in our feelings, needs, and desires? Or in our hearts, do we feel a need to act, or learn to act, so that those in our circle of influence are empowered, inspired, and included?

As I was researching skills, empathy was at the top of the list to include as a breakthrough skill and an integral part of the how you feel domain. Empathy is defined as having the capacity to understand and share the feelings of others. One way to think of empathy is to put ourselves in the shoes of others to grasp better how they feel, think, and, consequently, why they act in a specific manner.

But, I struggled with adding empathy as a breakthrough skill and including it as part of the CYA. It's not that I don't believe it isn't an essential soft skill. My point of view is that just showing empathy is not enough as a leader anymore.

> *Tough Talk*
> *Empathy helps you to understand and share in the feelings of others. But is it enough?*

Putting yourself in another's shoes to understand how they feel doesn't matter unless you take action in support of them. The call to action and the achievement of personal action is the difference between having compassion and just showing empathy.

If you see someone physically hurting due to an injury, you feel empathy toward their situation. You can most likely relate to physical hurt. But, most of us take no further action beyond showing empathy. On the other hand, a compassionate person takes action and aids in the healing process. That action could be as simple as offering over-counter pain relief, helping with household chores as they heal, or sitting with them at the hospital. The possibilities to show compassion are endless when there is an injury and pain.

You see, a young student is struggling to read a book. With empathy, you might relate to the student's situation and have strong feelings for them but do nothing more. Whereas a compassionate person sits with them and helps the student read.

These examples show the opportunity to choose compassion over empathy but might not relate to your workplace.

You are a peer leader on your team, and you see a co-worker struggling while giving a presentation in front of your boss and the rest of the team. They do not forgive and openly assault your co-worker with questions, pointed comments, and negatively slanted feedback that is not received well.

In your heart, you feel sorry for your peer. But do your feelings stop there? If so, you are feeling empathy towards their situation.

Or do you show compassion?

Perhaps, you spoke up in the meeting by pointing out some areas you felt were valuable information. Then, you show compassion by volunteering to offer your co-workers help in preparing their next presentation.

Can you recognize the difference? If not, here is a second example that illustrates the contrast between empathy and compassion.

Your company performs an annual employee satisfaction survey. For the third straight year, your department scores low on the questions asking if employees feel included in decisions and if they understand how their job relates to the corporate strategy.

Since this is the third straight year of a low score, you feel the need to take action. You scheduled a time to meet and speak with an employee council. They are open and forthcoming with their feelings and articulate examples supporting the annual survey's conclusions. As you listen, you remember being in their shoes as an employee before becoming a manager and then a director.

Empathy overwhelms you.

But coming out of that council meeting, do you act? Do you follow through with actions intended to improve employee participation in decisions, and how do your employees relate to the organization's strategy? Again, do you see and understand the difference?

Compassion is action-driven by empathy.

It is only through feelings of compassion that we recognize the need to take action and improve the world and the lives of those in our circle of influence.

This chapter will cover the actions you can take as a peer and leader in your organization to go beyond empathy and learn how to show compassion by taking action.

Lesson 17 - Learning How to Show Compassion

What you should take from this quote is that compassionate actions benefit everyone.

Learning how to be compassionate requires only one word. Action.

Opportunities to be compassionate present themselves every day. Most are obvious, a few might be hidden from sight, and a small handful might require considerable effort. To learn this breakthrough skill, you must look for ways to act to benefit others. Your goal in the workplace should be that you are part of the solution, not just a voice that points to the problem, nor just an ear that the words of others fall on.

At the core of compassion is to think big but start small. Focus on those who are in your circle of influence. These individuals rely on your leadership, your participation in the team, and those close to you who could use an uplifting hand. Even small acts of compassion go a long way in improving the workplace.

Here are the top 4 benefits of workplace compassion:

- You will personally realize improved interpersonal relationships.
- Employees will have a higher level of commitment and loyalty.
- This will lead to Increased execution and productivity in the workplace.
- All are resulting in higher customer engagement.

Here are the five foundational skills you need to learn, apply, and refine to start acting with compassion:

1. Be an active listener

The first foundational skill is to become an active listener. Of all the tips and tricks there are to improve individual listening skills, here are my favorites:

- Start with creating a safe environment for open discussion and sharing of thoughts.
- The next tip is to make good use of non-verbal clues. The biggest recommendation I can give you is to put down your phone or turn away from your technology when having a face-to-face conversation. If you are working virtually, then turn on your

camera during meetings and focus on being present by being attentive.

- You will need to make sure to maintain eye contact. This will show the speaking party that you are actively listening to.
- And last, as you listen, ask questions better to understand the other person's point of view, discover meaning, and clarify grey areas. Follow-up questions are a great way to demonstrate active listening.

2. Link the breakthrough skill of Emotional Intelligence

The next skill you will need is the emotional intelligence to accept disagreements and differing opinions.

Here you will link the breakthrough skills of compassion and emotional intelligence by accepting disagreements with peers or leaders and the opinions they might have. Compassion might require you to act when you don't fully understand or agree with a situation, but as a leader, you are called upon to do so.

3. Link the breakthrough skill Inclusion

To be truly compassionate, you will need to demonstrate acceptance openly. Acceptance is not just the reception of a person's characteristics but their ideas, opinions, and actions. Broaden your horizons by being inclusive. You will need to link this critical breakthrough skill as you learn to act with compassion.

4. Set others up for success

My favorite way to show compassion is to understand the intentions of others and work to help them open doors or remove barriers. Everyone has dreams, ambitions, and goals. You can act compassionately by learning these and assisting a person in achieving them. This will require you to take action by putting in the time to understand their intentions.

To do this, start by asking those around you these questions:

1. What do you want for yourself?
2. What do you want for your life?
3. What do you have to offer the world?

As you listen to the responses to these questions, ask yourself, how can I help this person achieve what they want? This will undoubtedly be an action that you will need to take. Follow through with it to open a door or remove a barrier so that they can flourish.

5. Be kind towards yourself

Last, be compassionate towards yourself. Avoid negative self-degradation. Seek opportunities to follow your dreams. Be bold and open with those who can show you compassion and act to your benefit. Find possibilities in all aspects of work that could potentially aid you in building personal and professional happiness.

Lesson 18 - Communicating Compassionately

I have defined compassion as an action driven by empathy. The most utilized action that shows compassion is communication. How you choose to communicate, and your actual message are all extremely vital to your effectiveness in showing compassion.

During this lesson, I discuss the basics of compassionate communication. As you learn these skills, make sure to use them every day. They are transferable across your professional and personal life to help enrich relationships.

In the last lesson on how to show compassion, I introduced some ways to improve listening. As a reminder, here are the four tips again:

- Start with creating a safe environment for open discussion and sharing of thoughts.
- The next tip is to make good use of non-verbal clues. The biggest recommendation I can give you is to put down your phone or turn away from your technology when having a face-to-face conversation. If you are working virtually, then turn on your

camera during meetings and focus on being present by being attentive.

- You will need to make sure to maintain eye contact. This will show the speaking party that you are actively listening to.
- And last, as you listen, ask questions better to understand the other person's point of view, discover meaning, and clarify grey areas. Follow-up questions are a great way to demonstrate active listening.

No Brainer
Why do you think I put the same content on improving listing twice in this workbook?
Because it's important!

I wanted to show these tips again because they are the foundation of communicating with compassion. If you are perceived as a poor listener by those who need your compassion, you are not maximizing your effort. Along with the tips we have just shared, there are a few other ways to improve listening with compassion.

Set aside and use the dedicated time to listen. Schedule one-on-ones with peers, direct reports, and your boss to have an open dialogue or discuss a topic that is already known. Drop into meetings unannounced or stop by and spend a few minutes with a person when you see them getting coffee or water in the break room.

Note: When working remotely, use messaging tools such as Slack, Teams, or other chat applications to stay connected and check in with your teammates. A simple, "hey, how's your day going?" can go a long way.

If you don't make time to listen, it will appear rushed and not genuine.

Next, understand when conversations need to be listened to in private or when conversations need to be heard in public. There is a difference. A great rule of thumb is that if the conversation is personal, make sure it's private. If the conversation affects or has a broad impact on others, it should be public, and every potential person who could be impacted should participate.

Another tip to improve listening is to restate what you have heard using your own words. This will show the other person you are intently listening to them and confirm your understanding of the conversation. This is extremely important when the conversation is complex, or there is much passion in the person's voice. Here are a couple of good phrases of how to do this:

"I think I understand what you are saying, but let me say it back to you just to make sure I fully understand."

"What I think I heard you say was…."

After you have listened effectively, compassionate communication doesn't stop there. You will need to respond. Your immediate response to the conversation is critical. Here is what I mean by your subsequent reaction is essential.

You have just listened to a peer expressing discord and dissatisfaction about a situation at work. The way you respond will illustrate one of three emotions:

- You don't care.
- You are capable of showing empathy.
- You are compassionate.

Here are examples of what those would look like from the words you could respond with. You actively listen to your peer's concerns and reply with the following:

This first response shows you don't care.

"This doesn't sound like a good situation, but I am unsure how I could help."

Or perhaps your response shows empathy but puts any potential action back on the other person.

"I am so sorry to hear this. You are right; it doesn't sound like a good situation. What are you going to do?"

The last example of a response is the start of compassionate action. You are offering or volunteering to help.

"I am so sorry to hear this. You are right; it doesn't sound like a good situation. What can I do to help?

This slightest change of just a few words alters the entire meaning of the response. The difference in words also indicates if you want to act with compassion or listen with empathy.

No Brainer
When in any conversation, you see an opportunity to show compassion, listen first, and then respond with an offer to help, a commitment of support, or an action you will take.

By applying these simple techniques for listening and responding with compassion, you will move away from just having empathy in your communication. You can make great strides towards compassionate action by leveraging improved communication skills.

Lesson 19 - How to Support a Teammate Through Stress

How can you support a co-worker who is suffering from work-related stress?

We fundamentally understand that stress harms productivity, culture, and team cohesion. It is also associated with a plethora of health problems in individuals. The origins of stress can be job-related or brought into the workplace by personal pressures and triggers. Regardless of its origins, as a co-worker and leader, you should know how to recognize it and utilize different techniques to reduce it.

Important Note: I use the term reduce it, not eliminate it. I recommend that anyone struggling with stress speak with a medical professional to stop it.

With that said, recognizing coworkers suffering from it and taking proactive steps to create an environment that minimizes stressors are activities everyone can and should be doing.

To get started, let's look at the top signs that a co-worker is feeling stressed:

- You might see a change in their everyday behaviors and attitude.
- They might have outbursts or socially withdraw from everyone.
- Unexplained and serial tardiness
- They are having trouble concentrating.
- A reduction in productivity
- Body language or a change in body language can also be a sign.
- Changes in their hygiene or outfits they wear at work.
- Frequent taking of personal time off

You will commonly notice multiple occurrences or a combination of any of these signs.

If you see any of these signs, it is clear that support and compassionate action are needed. Here are steps to support a co-worker or a direct report dealing with work-related stress.

Step 1: Acknowledge it privately

The first step you must take is privately recognizing it with the individual and helping them acknowledge they are suffering from stress. By acknowledging it with them, they become aware that others notice, and you become an ally.

You must understand how critical this conversation could be for the person struggling with stress.

Managers make the biggest mistake when approaching this private conversation by bringing up the topic and generically asking, "Is everything ok?"

Years ago, a manager noticed that I was struggling with work-related stress and approached me after a team meeting by saying, "Hey Chris, are you ok? You don't seem like yourself today."

He intended to be supportive, but his approach and timing gave me only one good option to respond with at that moment. I replied, "Yeah, just having an off day."

The conversation went no further.

The fact was that I was severely struggling with an assignment. I was losing sleep, not eating well, and was short-tempered towards everyone in my life. My co-workers, friends, and family were all feeling the effects of my stress. And it wasn't fair to any of them.

In retrospect, if my manager had approached me differently, I could have gotten better support and relief from the stress negatively impacting my mental health.

Here is how that conversation should have gone:

In the safety of a private office, my manager should have provided specific examples of how he had noticed the increase in my stress, the observed impacts it was having on me in the office, and a solution or two to help me.

"Hey, Chris, thanks for meeting with me. I wanted to speak with you about a couple of things that I've noticed and wanted to work through them together. Is now a good time to chat?"

After I confirm that I am good to have the conversation, he would continue with specific observations of the negative impacts and provide me with options to reduce my stress.

"Over the last couple of weeks, I have noticed a change in how you act, and I believe it's related to how stressed you are. During meetings, you are not your usual optimistic self. Instead, you are short with the team and make it clear to everyone that you have more important things to do."

"I know this isn't you, and if I had to guess, it is because you are stressed out with the assignment you have been working on. It is a big ask and takes up most of your time. I think we need to either get you help on the assignment or move a few other tasks off your plate, so you have less to worry about. What do you think? Is this a fair assessment?"

In just a few moments, my manager would have shown compassion for my situation, given me an example of what he had noticed, and then given a couple of suggestions we could discuss. As you can see, this is a much more effective way to approach a private discussion on stress with someone versus just asking, "Is everything ok?"

No Brainer
Make sure to suggest that they seek the advice of a medical professional if
they indicate a high level of stress impacting their health and well-being.

Step 2: Provide options

Next, suggest ways for them to reduce their stress level. Note, if you are their direct manager, you can help by taking proactive action to remove potential stressors.

The best two ways an individual can reduce stress caused by work are to either alter the way they work or how they interact with co-workers:

Here are some great ways anyone can alter how they work to reduce stress:

- Start by Prioritizing or de-prioritizing tasks and activities you are responsible for.
- Next, resist perfectionism in work.
- Make sure to apply clean delegation on tasks and decision-making authority.
- Work with others to find compromise and win-win situations.
- You should break larger projects and tasks into smaller ones and use a checklist to show progress.
- A great way to alter how you work is to stop over-committing yourself. Learn how to say no.
- Changing your work hours can improve your productivity and reduce stress.
- One of my favorites is to take regular breaks where you go for a walk or do another form of exercise.

To reduce stress levels for some individuals, you must change how and whom you interact with at work. Here are a few ways to do this.

- The biggest key is to avoid negativity and those who spread it.
- Always make sure to deal with conflict positively.
- Make building healthy, professional relationships a personal goal.

- A perfect way to reduce stress is to stop running with the same crowd of people.

Tough Talk
In some cases, as a leader, you might need to link courage by taking more decisive action in reassignment or corrective action to support a team member struggling with stress.

These are all ways you can reduce your stress level at work, or they can be suggestions you give to a coworker or a direct report.

Warning
The key is to do this one-on-one in a private discussion. Never in a meeting or when others are present.

Step 3: Keep an eye on the person

The last step is for you to continue monitoring the struggling person. Let them know when you see positive progress. If you don't see improvement, ask them again to speak with a medical professional or leverage any mental health resources your organization offers.

Suppose things start to deteriorate for that person, and they are not trying to improve. In that case, you should take action by alerting a manager higher in the organization or a human resource professional. Present your observations and any suggestions you have given in support of your co-worker.

Work-related stress can cause significant harm to an individual's physical and mental health. Acting with compassion in aid of a co-worker or direct report who is stressed is a true sign of leadership that goes way beyond just showing empathy.

Lesson 20 - The Traits of a Compassionate Leader

Now that you have learned some foundational soft skills to move from empathy to compassion, you will pull it all together to discuss how you can become a compassionate leader in this lesson.

Let's begin with how leadership is evolving. Trends in academic and industry literature using authenticity and humility to describe desired leadership traits have soared over the last decade.

Visit your favorite brick-n-mortar bookstore or glance at an online retailer. You will find numerous business and leadership books that list the common traits needed to lead with humility. These books attempt to teach you how to be an authentic leader. The growth and need for enhanced soft skills, such as humility and being authentic, are not likely to change anytime soon.

We need to look at its origins and identify what's driving it to understand this trend. The main factor pushing soft skill development in leadership is primarily changing dynamics within the workforce. Baby boomers are retiring, and millennials have quickly become its most prominent age group.

Along with the changing demographics, the influences placed on leaders to revise their leadership styles are under pressure. There is extreme pressure for change with how this new workforce wants to be led. Executives and senior leaders sitting in a centralized ivory tower passing down mandates that come out of closed-door strategy sessions are becoming a thing of the past.

To remain relevant, stay ahead of market trends, and react just in time to fend off competitors, leaders have to have their finger on the pulse of their employees and customers to be responsive to their needs with quick action. No longer can leaders ignore the pressure or just use lip service until it passes. With the growing awareness of the changing workforce dynamics, leaders at all levels have to learn a new skill; compassion.

No longer can a small team manager, a division vice president, or a CEO just empathize with employee or customer needs, concerns, and challenges. They now have to identify, understand, and respond with compassionate action.

Take the actions of major corporations over the last several years.

We have seen the sporting goods retail giant Dick's Sporting Goods get out of the lucrative firearm business, and even Wal-Mart changed how they sell firearm products in the wake of mass shootings. Social media giants feel massive pressure to take action concerning several social issues. An excellent example of how corporate leaders act with compassion is that more than 70% of the US-based Fortune 500 companies now offer extended leave for both men and women for the birth or adoption of a child.

Twenty years ago, maybe even just a decade ago, these actions would not have been considered. Yet, alone taken.

While these are great examples of how large organizations are starting to lead with compassion, the reasons you should coach your team with it are just as impressive.

Organizational benefits when a leader is compassionate include:

- Increased employee engagement
- Increased trust between leaders and employees
- Higher levels of accountability, flexibility, and grown transparency from both leaders and employees
- Improved individual performance
- Improved customer satisfaction
- Faster revenue and profitability growth

No Brainer
Learning to lead with compassion is just as important as a foundational skill to your success, whether running a multi-billion-dollar company, a nonprofit, or a small team.

As you review the lessons that make up this learning path and those that are part of the CYA, remember that you must apply and refine your new skills to improve.

Chapter 15
Courage

COURAGE in the face of adversity and fear is a very tough prospect to learn and apply.

Yes. You can learn how to be courageous and apply it safely in the workplace. Most of us associate courage as an emotion, not a skill. Yet courage is a noun defined as our ability to do something we are afraid of. Since courage is an ability, root skills can be learned, applied, and refined.

When creating the CYA, courage was the last skill to be included. There was an internal debate on how an individual learns courage and applies it safely in the work environment. As I worked towards creating the lessons that make up this chapter, it became apparent that courage was a skill that was necessary for any person to stand-out among peers, take calculated risks, and do amazing things.

To get started, let us redefine courage. Courage is a skill in which one takes deliberate action to promote ideas, equality, and improve performance. For example:

You are showing courage by recognizing you have a soft skill gap and are taking action to learn, apply, and refine new knowledge.

The employee who spoke up after they witnessed a peer stumble through a presentation and then publicly offered them help is an example of linking courage with compassion.

Seeing an opportunity at work and taking the initiative to act first and without direction shows courage and links this skill with entrepreneurial and execution mindsets.

To demonstrate courage, you need to learn how to do the following:

- Ask questions instead of making statements. Seek understanding and clarity first
- Speak succinctly with candor at all times. Demonstrate mastery over your emotions at all times
- Slow down and take time to get input from others and be open to different points of view
- Be bold, be assertive, and openly suggest other, better ways to work
- Insist on using data to make rational and informed decisions
- Take the initiative when you see an opportunity or issue that others might be blind to or have tried and failed at in the past.
- Know when to stand up for your convictions and points of view in the face of rejection
- Don't let yourself be bogged down with wasteful tasks; learn to say no.

Have you ever heard the quote: "Fortune favors the bold?" This Latin proverb means that courage in action and taking calculated risks can lead to good fortune. The last way to demonstrate courage at work is to think big.

During this chapter, you will learn different tips and techniques for how you can show courage at work. These include how and when to speak up, be candid and direct, coach, and have tough conversations with peers, employees, and even your boss.

Lesson 21 - How to have Radical Candor With Everyone (Even your Boss)

Let's learn to show courage at work with some great tips to keep in mind when speaking. The first lesson you need to know in showing courage in the workplace is to be straightforward and candid when speaking. All other acts of courage are built by your ability to communicate with candor and clarity. This does not mean that you should be rude, overly direct, or speak from an emotional state. Speaking with candor means you talk with fairness, honesty, simplicity, and sincerity.

To be successful while speaking with candor is to find a balance between the words you say and how you deliver them. All aspects of communication must be considered: tone, body language, timing, audience, and especially your words.

To learn how to be candid at work, follow these seven tips:

Tip 1: Start with clarity of purpose

Are you making a point during a disagreement, providing a suggestion, or speaking out against a wrong? Purpose in speaking allows you to frame your conversation and words.

Tip 2: Know the emotional triggers that could be present in the conversation

For example, if a manager is passionate about an idea, calling it out in the middle of a meeting might pull an emotional trigger. Instead, identify another time to speak with candor about how you feel about their idea.

Tip 3: Check your assumptions

You will usually press against normal boundaries and possibly the organizational culture by speaking up. Before you stick your neck out, ensure your assumptions and thoughts have been verified as accurate.

Tip 4: Think win-win in every situation

Focus on the positive outcomes for the organization, not individual ones. By staying focused on positive organizational development, no one will be able to question your motives.

Tip 5: Make sure to consider the perspectives and opinions of others

They, too, might be trying to speak with candor, and your ability to listen and be considerate of their point of view will elevate your own.

Tip 6: Organize your thoughts and back up your key points with specifics and examples

Many people believe that being courageous and having candor in a conversation is the person with the loudest voice. It doesn't. Candor is more about organizing your thoughts versus being loud with them.

> *Tough Talk*
> *Have you noticed that I mentioned specifics and examples when having tough conversations? See Lesson 19 on Helping a Teammate Through Stress and the next Lesson in this chapter on Coaching up.*

I have mentioned this a couple of times because we often jump into a critical discussion with a peer, direct report, or manager without specific examples that provide the evidence the other person needs to hear.

Tip 7: Use the words "We" and "Our." Not "I," "Me," or "My"

And, definitely never use statements that start with "you." For example:

"We have an opportunity to learn." Sounds a hell of a lot better than saying, "you have an opportunity to learn." "Our team will benefit" is better than saying, "My team will benefit."

When you are learning to be candid while speaking, you are also learning how to get and keep others engaged in your conversation and ultimately side with your point of view or perspective. Remember, if you are having a candid conversation, you have a different opinion, a different solution, or idea, or you might be calling out something you see as wrong or not equitable.

No Brainer
If others already side with you, there is no reason to be courageous and have a candid conversation.

Lesson 22 - Courage in Coaching Up

Having tough conversations in the workplace requires courage. It requires even more when you must coach up and provide constructive feedback to your immediate manager. The art of coaching your manager requires you to learn, develop self-efficacy, and demonstrate it where others are afraid to speak up.

Managers are in a challenging role. Their job is to coach and develop employees to get the most out of them to achieve organizational objectives.

Tough Talk
Being a people manager doesn't exclude someone from needing coaching for themselves. I would argue that people manager needs more coaching than their employees.

However, we must better understand most individual managers' knowledge and limitations. Managers face three immense challenges.

First, most line managers were promoted into leadership roles simply for being high-performing direct contributors, which is part of the second challenge.

In most cases and organizations, newly promoted individuals attend training or manager orientation, but they never learn the root skills needed to be successful people managers. Most management training is dominated by conceptual knowledge and only partially addresses soft skills through awkward, unrealistic role-playing.

The third challenge is that managers rarely receive meaningful and timely feedback on their skills and ability to lead others. In today's fast-paced, often remote working environment, senior managers, or up-line managers, are not present to see the actions of their direct reports. By not being present or having very little presence, up-line managers miss the opportunity to give line managers, who are their direct reports, mean-ingful feedback that improves their performance.

Tough Talk
The lack of top-down coaching for managers is why it is vital that peers or a manager's direct reports dare to coach up.

While this lesson is intended to help you learn how to give your manager constructive feedback and coaching, these six tips can also be used for any difficult conversation at work.

Tip 1: Identify the development opportunity your manager has

This opportunity will always relate to soft skills, such as interactions, emotional intelligence, or the manager's self-efficacy.

Warning
Don't focus on their development gap; instead, focus on its effects on you, the team, and the business outcomes.

Tip 2: Properly frame the conversation you want to have and anticipate potential outcomes

This will help you practice the conversation and anticipate the different reactions your manager could have.

Tip 3: Pick your moment

After identifying the opportunity, framing the conversation, and practic-ing, you must pick your moment. It needs to be in private. Never in public.

In picking your moment, leverage your situational awareness to ensure that you are not trying to have a difficult conversation during a stressful or emotionally heightened time for the manager.

No Brainer
When possible, have the conversation towards the end of the day. If the

discussion goes sideways, you both can go home at the end of the workday and regroup your thoughts.

Tip 4: Set the stage properly

The best way to do this is to ask them if now is a good time to talk about something you have noticed or observed.

Ensure you introduce the opportunity you have identified so the manager can prepare for the conversation. If there is hesitation, ask if you should schedule a time when they can be more prepared.

Tip 5: Choose your words carefully but don't shy away from having candor

Don't be wordy, don't sugarcoat the opportunity or its effects on you, the team, or the business. You are in the moment. Now is when you show courage.

> *Warning*
> *If you sidestep the issue, then you miss out on helping your manager make improvements.*

Tip 6: Focus on positive outcomes for your manager

This should not be an emotionally led or charged conversation. To keep it away from potentially negativity, or hard feelings, state the benefits of the manager's improvement and give concrete examples of when you have observed the gap.

Bonus Tip

While you have identified an opportunity and framed it by trying to think of all possible outcomes and reactions to the conversation, it is still possible that your manager doesn't receive the feedback well. If you have followed these tips and are confident that you have conveyed a sincere message focused on positive outcomes for your manager, then perhaps your manager is not ready to be coached.

This is not uncommon, especially for newly promoted managers or those with big egos. If this is the case, know when to end the conversation and gently move on.

A good statement to make when this is needed is: "My apologies for possibly speaking out of place. I intended to help you {insert the opportunity}, not to overstep."

Lesson 23 - How to Speak, Present, and Interact with Executives

Does anyone get nervous when speaking with an executive?

I used to. But I learned how to show courage and created six essential rules you can follow when speaking or presenting to an executive. But before I give you the six rules.

Speaking with or presenting to senior managers and executives takes courage. Sometimes your message might not be what they want to hear, or your words can turn into unintended actions.

On more than one occasion, I have witnessed an executive make major decisions because of a single presentation or a conversation with one opinionated person. It's true. In most cases, the loudest person in the room wins. If you are not the loudest person, you need your message conveyed, and you are not the loudest person in the room, it will be vital to display courage.

Similar to the lack of knowledge and the limitations that line managers have, executives, too, suffer from significant challenges. While their challenges are different from junior managers, they must still rely on others to be direct and candid with them.

Here are the top challenges that executives face:

1. Must rely on the candor of others

Most executives are not subject matter experts in everything. Most have risen to an executive role through a specific track (Finance, Marketing, Operations, etc.) They must rely on others, who are experts, to disseminate knowledge and give them open and honest data, perspectives, and

2. Lack of specific knowledge

Next, they have access to tons of big data but lack the knowledge of many crucial company processes, daily ways of working, and the everyday pain points employees and customers face.

Remember the iceberg of ignorance infographic shared in Chapter 10. This is an excellent representation of how executives might not be aware of all that goes on in their organization and how information doesn't always reach them.

Image 25: The Iceberg of Ignorance

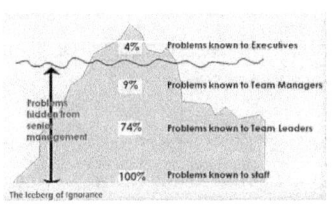

Source: Yoshida, S., (1989). *Quality improvement and TQC management at Calsonic in Japan and Overseas.*

3. Massive time restraints

The third challenge executives have is that time is of the essence for them. Their schedules are packed, and there is always something else they can be doing besides listening to you.

So, when it's your turn to speak or present your information to an executive, follow these simple six rules to show courage and wow everyone in the room!

Rule 1: Have complete confidence in what you are saying

There are two aspects to this. You can either have developed self-efficacy in your ability to speak with an executive, or you need to have complete conviction in what you are saying. If you still need the courage to talk with an executive, you haven't yet achieved self-efficacy. So, you need to believe in the words coming out of your mouth entirely.

Rule 2: Less is always more

Don't use 12 words when five will do. Don't linger on negative points; don't read directly from a PowerPoint slide if you are presenting. Simply state the key takeaways or facts and any supporting evidence or recommendations you have.

Rule 3: Get to the point

If you have a recommendation for the executive or a decision you need for them to make, then start with that. For example, if you have a recommendation and give a presentation, your opening slide should be the recommendation followed by the data to support it. Get to the point you need to make quick and use your presentation for supporting evidence.

> *Warning*
> *Don't spend all your time presenting data; only get to your recommendation in the closing minutes of the meeting or conversation. There will be no time for questions, decision-making, or next steps.*

Rule 4: Be an expert, not another opinion

You are speaking of making a recommendation. Make sure it is based on your knowledge and insight. Not something that you are unfamiliar with. Most individuals who get into difficult situations when speaking or presenting to an executive venture into areas of the business or knowledge that are not their expertise.

> *No Brainer*
> *It's ok to say, "I don't know." For example, if you work in marketing and are asked about depreciation on a capital asset, it's ok to say, "I don't know." But make sure to add, "if you would like, I can find out."*

Rule 5: Make sure your data is accurate

You should always be prepared to answer pointed questions and ensure your data is accurate. Sound executives are data wizards and can quickly spot errors or missing information. Double and even triple-check your numbers if you are presenting or speaking to data.

Make sure everything is correct before you share it. When you get asked a question, answer it directly and stay focused on the question. Don't try to talk about something that wasn't requested.

Rule 6: Don't step in it

Don't try to bullshit executives. Leave the BS in another room and don't waste their time.

> *Warning*
> *They can spot it a mile away, and you can quickly lose your credibility, atten-*
> *tion, and opportunity to wow them.*

As you learn and apply these rules, you will develop self-efficacy in speaking with executives, and the level of courage you will need to act will be reduced. Like any other action, once you successfully do it a few times, you will get the hang of it.

Lesson 24 - How to Show Courage in Decision Making

None of the daily activities require more of the 12 breakthrough skills from the CYA than the act and responsibility of decision-making.

We know that excellent decision-making requires emotional intelligence, critical thinking, compassion, interactions with others, and inclusivity. But, did you also know that many decisions need you to have and show courage more than any other skill in your architecture?

Do you decide to speak up when you see injustice or inequality at work? The decision to leave a job to start your own company requires significant courage. Or what about the courage you need in deciding to coach up when you see your manager needs support because they have a blind spot?

These few examples each require that you dare to act and follow through. During this lesson, we will center the discussion on making tough decisions. Not simple, everyday decisions.

Instead, that consequential risk-taking that affects your reputation impacts others and can influence your career. Here is a quick story about the courage needed in decision-making.

In October 1945, President Harry S. Truman received a gift from a friend, and it resided on the Resolute Desk in the Oval Office until Truman left it in 1953. That gift was a simple wooden sign that read "the buck stops here." The expression comes from the slang "pass the buck," which simply means to pass the responsibility to another person.

President Truman had made several consequential decisions about ending the second world war with Japan just months earlier. He felt it was his duty as a leader not to pass the buck but rather make the decision and carry the weight of its burden.

While none of us will be in the situation that President Truman found himself in August of 1945, we are likely at some point going to have to make consequential decisions that will affect our lives or those of others.

How you approach these situations, how you leverage data, and your ability to execute or influence others will be decided by your courage to make the toughest of decisions. Like other skills, you can develop courage when facing difficult decisions.

Here are some tried and tested strategies for showing courage in action to make big decisions:

Strategy 1: Follow your intuition

An important strategy is following your intuition and listening to your inner wisdom when making tough decisions. If you feel strongly one way or the other, that is likely to be the right direction.

> *Warning*
> *Know the difference between emotional and rational inner voices. Emotional ones will not lead you to the right decision.*

Strategy 2: Use Data and pull in others

The best way to remove emotions from big decisions is to leverage data and invite others to provide insights, perspectives, and recommendations. Please don't go down the road of analysis paralysis, but don't make big decisions without objectively examining any data related to it.

Strategy 3: Be the decision-maker

Don't be fooled; consensus is not decision-making.

Remember, the buck stops with you as a leader! Not a team that provided you with advice. It is best to listen to differing opinions while exploring all alternatives for big decisions, but the responsibility resides with you.

It's natural to want others to agree and swiftly support your decisions. But don't waste too much effort getting others to agree with you. Instead, make the decision and use your time and energy to get them to buy in after it's made. Surprisingly, this approach is much easier.

Strategy 4: Understand the landscape

The following strategy is to weigh the potential benefits and risks of the decision. This implies that you will utilize your critical thinking skills to evaluate alternatives. Part of this exercise is also to visualize possible outcomes and the odds of achieving each.

Suppose your desired benefit only has a ten percent chance of being achieved. In that case, you might need to go in a different direction with your decision—the odds of a successful outcome matter when weighing a decision's potential benefits and risks.

You will also need to fully understand your decision's down and upstream and immediate and long-term ramifications. Here you pull in compassion by empathizing with how your decision will affect others, and then you act following what is best.

Strategy 5: Own It!

The last bit of advice, own the decision.

Especially if it has negative consequences or adversely impacts others.

In the introduction, I mentioned that I was once laid off and fired by the same company. The layoff came in 2008 when the United States economy turned sour. I was in direct sales, working towards management, and had just moved into a new role with a more extensive territory and much more visibility to senior leaders. And then, the housing market crashed, large banks crumpled, and my employer had to make a tough choice. I lost my job in a reduction of force (RIF) that impacted about 15% of the company's total sales force.

I understood the financials of the situation and the problematic place my employer was in. My wife, who had given birth to our second child a couple of months early, was less understanding.

If the decision has positive benefits and goes well, share the accolades with your team of trusted advisors who provided you with the data and insights.

These five strategies in showing courage in decision-making will improve your decisions' accuracy, speed, and impact. Make sure to employ them in your decisions so that you learn, apply, and refine them.

Chapter 16
Inclusive

THE BENEFITS of being inclusive in the workplace have been well-documented:

- Increased job satisfaction
- Higher productivity
- More creativity and innovation
- Accelerated speed to transform and improved individual adaptability
- Higher employee engagement and morale
- Better customer satisfaction
- Stronger employee retention
- Higher revenue and profitability growth

Why do most organizations still struggle to create an inclusive environment if the benefits are overwhelming?

Is it due to a lack of knowledge, lack of incentives, lack of strategy, or lack of execution?

Well, It's a little bit of all of the above. Most organizations try to improve inclusion by providing leaders with basic conceptual or factual knowledge (like the same facts I gave you). Be an inclusive leader, and as a leader, you can reap all these benefits!

Creating an inclusive team, workforce, and culture is not that simple. While improving knowledge about inclusion is a good step. Experience has shown that injecting a conceptual understanding among leaders is insufficient to improve inclusion.

The next mistake that many organizations make is approaching inclusion through diversity efforts. The most popular way is to offer executives and managers incentives to diversify their teams. The human resources department usually drives these programs to force diversity. The topic of diversity is essential, but the goal needs to create "inclusive" diversity. Not just changing the demographic makeup of a team or organization.

Warning
Diversity and inclusion are not the same things! Changing the demographics
of a team doesn't make a leader more inclusive. This chapter will teach you
the difference.

Another mistake is that most corporate strategies for improving inclusion are usually a top-down approach. Where I have witnessed organizations succeed in this area, do so by applying a bottom-up approach.

Last, execution to improve inclusion falls short because it is challenging to measure and define what success looks like. So, most leaders can simply check a diversity box and claim that they have improved inclusion by adding minorities to their teams with no evidence to show that this has increased inclusion.

We must change how we approach inclusion as a society, as organizations, and as individuals.

We shouldn't look at it as just conceptual knowledge a person can gain, hoping it leads to improved actions and outcomes. Instead, we need to view it as an individual soft skill that can be learned, applied, and refined.

Inclusiveness is part of how you feel domain in the CYA because evidence shows that individuals who feel a need and a desire and can find purpose in including others are more likely to do so. I believe that if an individual changes the way they feel, not the way they think, about inclusion, they and their organizations will achieve the benefits listed at the top of this chapter. To help you develop and improve your inclusiveness skills, I have developed a set of lessons that will teach you how to become an inclusive leader and not only invite it but elevate it as part of your professional identity.

Lesson 25 - Treating Employees as People

Let me get straight to the point.

A root cause of why we struggle to include others and create an environment and culture of inclusiveness is that we forget to treat employees as people. We forget that they have opinions, feelings, experiences, and education. Most importantly, when omitted, we forget they have cause to be concerned about, especially if things go sideways.

Here are the top complaints of employees concerning inclusion:

- The most common is that employees feel they are not part of the decision-making process.
- For example, they are not consulted when senior leaders set major planning or strategic direction.
- Information and data are hoarded and not shared openly with them.
- Not part of the organizational goal-setting and employee expectation processes
- Many employees feel that leaders are uninformed. Meaning that they are detached from day-to-day activities and lack the knowledge of what happens and the everyday challenges employees face
- Employees are frustrated when they don't have enough say in their personal development.
- And last, the overall lack of transparency regarding why and when impactful decisions are made.

The list can go on. But, as an employee, what complaints would you add? Are there any that stand out to you from your own experiences? I have a couple from my personal experiences that I used to complain about.

So, why do organizational leaders not treat employees as people? Part of it is psychological. Many leaders believe that they are all-knowing, have all the answers and all the information that is needed and that it is their job to take action. You might refer to this as ego. The other part of why leaders don't treat employees as people is that they don't have the know-how.

Yes, that might sound kind of funny. But have you ever had a conversation with an executive that felt awkward? Like they were from Saturn, and you were from Mercury? It might have felt like you didn't have much in common other than being in the same solar system. This is the human part that we forget.

If you felt awkward, it is safe to assume they did too! So imagine if a simple break room or elevator conversation is awkward; how would it feel for them to stop and ask your opinion on an upcoming decision? Or to invite you to a meeting and ask you to contribute. The reality is that their planetary orbit and yours might be light-years apart. To treat each other as people, both organizational leaders and employees need to take action to close that orbit and establish a positive rapport. Here's how:

First, let's talk about how employees can extend their orbit and improve inclusiveness. Because as an employee, you, too, need to take action toward the leader to help create inclusion.

> *Tough Talk*
> *Don't be fooled into thinking that inclusion is just the responsibility of leadership and skill they should learn, apply, and refine. You, as an employee, have a considerable part to play in improving inclusion.*

Employee Tip 1: Don't contribute to the negativity

The first tip for an employee is not to speak negatively about peers and the leaders in your organization. How do you feel when someone talks about you behind your back? It is not a good feeling, and this immature behavior does not help create an inclusive culture.

> *Warning*
> *Contrary to what you might think, many leaders know precisely who speaks ill of them and are often aware of negative comments and feelings.*

Employee Tip 2: Find your voice

As an employee, you need to be bold, which means that you should be open and forthcoming about your opinions, desires, and recommendations. You have to link your newly learned courage skills! Boldness is tact, discipline, situational awareness, and passion. Show leaders these root skills, and you will start getting invited to meetings and asked about decisions you would not have otherwise been included in.

Employee Tip 3: Find ways to stand out

Look for ways to go above and beyond by being part of an employee council, a diversity group, or out-of-work activities such as the company softball team, book club, or bowling league. If none of these exist, then take the initiative by starting one. Increase your exposure to individuals outside your usual circle. This is super important in helping to improve your inclusion.

Be a leader and set a positive example for others to follow.

Employee Tip 4: Take a lesson from a Hall of Fame Football Coach

Apply the Bobby Bowden rule to interactions.

Hall of Fame college football coach Bobby Bowden once said that when he meets someone for the first time, he makes it a point to keep 98% of the conversation on the other person. Not about himself.

This shows the person you are interested in and invested in what they have to say during this conversation. Don't use this time to talk about yourself. Everyone loves to talk about themselves. Allow them to speak by asking questions, showing active listening skills, and following this great rule!

Let's switch gears and talk about how, as a leader, you can improve inclusion with your team and within your organization.

Leader Tip 1: Start with what matters most

Start with the decision-making process. If you recall the top employee complaints regarding inclusion, most had to deal with being included during decision-making.

To improve, I encourage you to invite others into the process by asking them to provide data, opinions, and recommendations.

> *No Brainer*
> *Gently remind them that you ultimately hold the decision rights, but their*
> *input is important, and you will consider it.*

This might feel weird initially, but your team will learn how to better provide you with their data, opinions, and recommendations. Over time, the quality of their inputs will improve, but this will also help build an inclusive team culture. Imagine the power of developing your team's critical thinking skills while simultaneously enhancing inclusion. Wow! That would be very valuable to your organization.

Leader Tip 2: Delegate

We are staying with the crucial topic of decision-making. A second way to improve inclusion is to identify areas where decisions can be pushed down to the lowest possible level in the organization and then shift the responsibility to that level.

Give employees the right to make decisions during their work and the items that most affect their job. Don't hoard decision-making rights if others can do it quicker, with more information and more at stake. The clean delegation will improve inclusion because you treat employees as people by simply trusting them to do their jobs.

> *No Brainer*
> *This is an excellent opportunity to evaluate the decisions you, as a leader,*
> *have to make using a modified Eisenhower Matrix that plots decisions, not*
> *the tasks you are responsible for.*

Leader Tip 3: Provide an opportunity and forum

Set up a council or employee-led team that helps keep the pulse on the needs and emotions of their fellow employees. Ask employees to set up, volunteer, or figure out a way to create this council themselves.

You don't pick who is on it or how big it is. Give your employees complete control and encourage them to create a team charter that describes its purpose, values, and meeting cadence. Then allow this newly formed council or employee-led team to decide on the topics covered and when to include you.

> *Tough Talk*
> *If you currently don't trust your team to create an employee council or if you are afraid of what they might say… Then you need this more than you know!*

Leader Tip 4: Actions speak louder than words

Don't proclaim that you are improving inclusion. Just take action.

The team doesn't need to hear what you want to do or what you want to accomplish. They have been craving action, so take it.

> *Warning*
> *Damn sure, don't send an email that proclaims that you are going to improve inclusion! If I hadn't seen it before, I wouldn't have to give you a warning NOT to do it.*

Leader tip 5: It's a two-way street

Remember the Bobby Bowden rule we discussed for how an employee can improve inclusion? It should be no surprise that the same rule applies to leaders.

It's ok to ask an employee, "how was your weekend?" Or, "What plans do you have this evening?" It is even better to ask, "What are your thoughts about {insert topic}?"

Learning how to small talk and carry on a conversation that doesn't seem awkward because the employee thinks you are evaluating or judging them will do a lot to boost openness and comfort.

Inclusiveness takes a strong focus and a bold willingness to learn new skills. Being an inclusive leader takes a commitment to action.

The tips shared in this lesson are all items that any individual, regardless of their role in an organization, can take towards learning how to be more inclusive. Pick the one or two that you feel would most help you and apply it. You need to have confidence and go for it! Otherwise, what is the point of learning how to be inclusive if you don't include your new knowledge in your efforts?

Lesson 26 - How Diversity of Thought will Improve Inclusion

Diversity of thought in decision-making, problem-solving, and strategic planning is one of the many benefits of inclusion in the workplace. Breaking down the barriers that prevent expanded participation and input from others who are usually excluded help to inject new thought, ideas, and energy into teams and organizations.

As I discussed in the lesson on treating employees like people, everyone wants to feel included and would like to be in the room where influential work is planned and decided on. While this can't become standard practice for every action and decision, it can become a part of how larger and more influential ones are done.

Let's look at an example that some of you might be familiar with.

Tons of research over the last three decades has shown that the success rate of IT projects achieving a return on investment through improved functionality and user adoption is less than 30%, which means that more than 70% of them don't deliver on the goals they set out to achieve. While there are many reasons why the failure rate is so high, most of them relate to end-users not being included in the collection of requirements, the building of the software, the testing, and the many decisions that are part of each of those processes.

This example is also true of so many other initiatives that organizations try. It is usual for leaders, possibly partnered with outside consultants, to look to make improvements, changes, or major overhauls, without including the voice of those who will be most impacted. Those individuals with the most knowledge about day-to-day challenges, pain points, and activities and those most responsible for the initiative's success are often left out. But, there are ways to improve the diversity of thought to become a more inclusive team and organization.

Commit and be consistent (your superpower)

Committing to it is the first thing you need to do to improve the diversity of thought. As an employee and leader, you have to make a firm personal decision to either be or not be inclusive. There is no half measure, no half steps. You have to take consistent action to be an inclusive leader, or your decision to be one will be empty. A simple way to start small is to suggest that your team tries something new as a way that breaks with your usual ways of doing things.

> *No Brainer*
> *Do you remember what Einstein said about insanity? Don't be insane!*

Listen intently and openly

Once you commit, you must be open to the diversity of thought by listening to others. At this point, you are linking other breakthrough skills from the CYA.

Specifically, emotional intelligence, courage, and compassion. Look for opportunities to invite others into the decision-making or planning process or find ways to get yourself invited into them within your organization. The point is not for you to decide; it is for you to offer your experiences and point of view by putting forth informed recommendations that others consider.

> *No Brainer*
> *Don't panic when it goes astray at first. Remember, becoming inclusive*

doesn't happen overnight and might go against years, possibly even decades, of historical normalcy.

Learn together as a team

As you learn, seek knowledge from outside your organization to improve and teach you and your team how to be more inclusive.

I have worked with several teams who leverage design thinking techniques when trying to solve a problem, make an important decision, or improve employee or customer experience. As you start injecting new knowledge, don't expect perfection with the diversity of thought quickly.

Remember, by building self-efficacy and mastery, you must learn, apply, and refine it to become your own.

Design thinking is a great tool to improve the diversity of thought in teams. Here are some great resources (many are free!):

- Ideo U - www.ideou.com/pages/design-thinking
- Stanford d School - www.dschool.stanford.edu/resources
- IBM - www.ibm.com/design/thinking/

Culture trumps strategy

The last way to improve the diversity of thought and inclusion within your team and your organization is to create an environment where it is celebrated. Don't just welcome different ideas, but rather celebrate them.

Work hard to develop a culture where you don't need a title to be a leader. Create a culture of openness, rejoicing, and learning from failure. The creation of culture needs to be supported by leadership, but the employees influence it the most at a grassroots level.

Warning
And yes, different small teams, groups, divisions, or departments can take on a sub-culture all to themselves. Don't be deterred if your organization doesn't promote diversity of thought and inclusion. You can still lead by example with your team and peers.

To become a more inclusive leader and strengthen this crucial break-through skill, you must prioritize improving thought diversity. Giving others a voice and listening to their point of view, opinions, and recommendations promote inclusivity.

Lesson 27 - The Art of Clean Delegation

Delegation is a simple concept but extremely difficult to do with significant effect.

Delegation of authority, responsibility, and decision-making rights is an art as it is a skill. To delegate, a person has to categorically trust the other party to act responsibly and achieve the same outcome for the delegated activity.

The many benefits of delegating authority are:

- It allows a leader to prioritize higher-value tasks.
- This can occur because it improves the leader's time management and productivity.
- The delegation has been shown to speed up and help organizations make better decisions.
- It creates a diversity of thought and action.
- Improves the engagement of those being given authority
- It is an excellent opportunity for individuals to learn and develop professionally.
- And last, it prepares the delegated person for career advancement in a safe environment.

The benefits are resoundingly positive. Yet, research also shows that several negative aspects can hinder delegation if not done correctly. These include:

- It becomes a training exercise rather than an effort to execute better. Because of this, it takes up more time than intended.
- A leading cause of delegation breaking down is poor communication when vague instructions or expectations are not fully conveyed.

- Next, the wrong person is selected as the delegated authority.
- A common mistake is that the delegating person expects perfection on the first pass.
- And last, when things go well, the recognition and accolades are not shared by the delegating person.

The biggest flaw in delegation is that it is not clean, which means it is dirty.

Dirty delegation is when a task or activity is given to another party, but the decision-making rights remain with the delegating person. Over the last decade, several research articles have each shown that almost three-quarters of all delegated tasks suffer from dirty delegation. The causes for dirty delegation center around trust and power. The delegating person doesn't fully trust the other party; more importantly, they are unwilling to give up control.

> *Warning*
> *Research shows that three-quarters of all delegated tasks suffer from dirty delegation.*

The latter reason, of not being willing to give up power, is the leading cause of why the delegation of authority is dirty. Once gained, power is infectious. Those who hold it feel special, hold ideological and political positions over others and do everything they can to maintain power. This is when the dirty delegation rises.

Here is a quick example of what I see the most. A leader is strapped for time; they conceptually know that to perform better and focus on higher-value tasks, they need to give away some activities to others. So, the leader picks a task with a high degree of associated work that they naturally expect the other person to do. Still, they don't allow that person to make correlating decisions related to the activity. Thus, the leader maintains power, and the benefits of the delegation are never truly realized.

Here are the top five ways to best delegate tasks cleanly and maximize their benefits.

1. Identify a task, a decision, or work that should be delegated

Focus on time-consuming, low-priority tasks. This is a great spot to link breakthrough skills by pulling up the Eisenhower matrix presented in the execution mindset and using it to help you identify the best tasks to delegate.

2. Be mindful of whom you choose

Make sure they can perform both the work and make the decisions required with minimal hand-holding from you. A tip here is to identify a person who is either a subject matter expert or working towards a promotion and advancing in their career.

3. Communicate effectively by making sure instructions and expectations are very clear

Breakdowns at this point often occur because communication and delegation are rushed, and no support is offered. Ensure the person taking on the new task has both the capability and that you have transferred all related knowledge and expectations to them. This will enable them to act and make decisions.

4. Make sure you follow up and check in on the progress being made

This isn't you stepping back in and taking over or making the decisions. This is you confirming that the person, who now owns the delegated activities, is progressing without issues and is learning how to do the work without your continued support and oversight.

5. Give credit where credit is due

Ensure that you publicly recognize the person who completed the activities when rewards and accolades are handed out. This gives them the feeling of appreciation, builds their confidence, and makes them look favorable towards you in delegating cleanly and giving credit to the right person. It's a classic win-win.

The last point I want to make on clean delegation is how you will know when it's been done well.

You will know that you have delegated authority correctly when you have identified the best tasks using your Eisenhower matrix and selected the right person(s) to delegate full authority to. Including decision-making rights.

You communicated well by transferring all relevant knowledge to them and following up to check their progress.

The last thing you have done is recognize their hard work by giving them the due accolades.

Once you have experienced all these, you have successfully applied clean delegation.

Chapter 17
Self-Efficacy

SELF-EFFICACY IS a term that originated in the late 1970s and was first used by psychologist Albert Bandura. Dr. Bandura researched human functionality and behavior when he published his theory on self-efficacy. He later published multiple works, including *Social Foundations of Thought and Action: A social cognitive theory.*

To summarize his conclusions, self-efficacy is individuals' belief about their capabilities to learn, perform, and complete a task to achieve a preferred outcome. Self-efficacy is a driving force behind an individual's motivation to start a task and see it through to a positive conclusion.

> *Tough Talk*
> *Unless people believe their capabilities and actions will yield their desired outcome, they are less likely to do it and persevere when challenges arise.*

Two quick points on self-efficacy.

While this term is common in education to describe the motivation and capabilities of students to learn and master new subjects, it is rarely understood and used outside of this field. My point of view is that self-efficacy is a core soft skill that every individual, regardless of profession, needs to learn, apply, and refine as they build their architecture.

The second point I want to make is that self-efficacy and confidence differ.

Yes, there are some parallels and similarities. But confidence is a feeling of self-assurance. It is believed that you will achieve a positive result, whereas self-efficacy is a motivational influence. For example, a confident salesperson will believe in their abilities to achieve a positive outcome without the necessary knowledge. But, a salesperson with self-efficacy will be motivated to start because they believe in their selling skills.

The difference is that when self-efficacy and confidence are at odds, you lack the confidence to achieve the desired outcome but have faith in your skill. Self-efficacy is more likely to determine your motivation and behavior.

This is why self-efficacy is a breakthrough skill part of the CYA, and confidence is a mindset and a by-product of developing self-efficacy.

I understand that I am not in a position to support you in developing self-efficacy for the work tasks you are responsible for. But I am in a position to help you build self-efficacy for the breakthrough skills that are most important for standing out among your peers and for continued career advancement.

During this chapter, you will be presented with both the conceptual and procedural knowledge you will need to develop in all aspects of your life, as well as the metacognitive knowledge needed to recognize when it is present and when it needs to be learned for a skill, a task, and how to identify it and coach it in others.

Lesson 28 - The 4 Sources of Self-Efficacy

As you learn how to create self-efficacy, the first step is to know where inspiration and information for it will come from. There are four primary sources where you, as an individual, will gather, observe, and analyze data while forming self-efficacy for a particular skill or task. They are:

1. Your experiences in the mastery of the skill
2. Vicariously seeing others perform the skill well
3. Social pressure or persuasion for the skill

4. Emotional reactions to a skill such as anxiety, stress, optimism, and confidence

The most influential source is your mastery of the skill

As we learn a new skill, we go through a learning curve from a slow beginning to rapid progression toward proficiency. At this proficiency stage, we have ultimately mastered the skill, and as a result, we form self-efficacy.

For example, critical thinking is one of the CYA's breakthrough skills as part of the how you think domain. As you learn the steps to mature your critical thinking, things will go slow at first. You might experience awkwardness, confusion, fear, and a desire to quit or abandon using this new skill. Through commitment and perseverance, you will achieve a breakthrough and realize rapid progression on how quickly you can apply these skills, and applying critical thinking becomes more effortless. During this time, your self-efficacy in being able to use critical thinking across multiple situations builds. Your experiences and mastery of a skill propel your self-efficacy.

Image 26: Commonly accepted learning curve for complex knowledge

The following source influencing your self-efficacy is witnessing or observing others performing the skill well

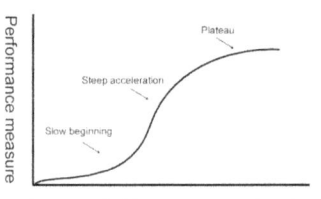

By vicariously observing how others approach, perform, and succeed at a skill, the more belief you gain in being able to mimic that capability on a high level. This is exceptionally true of young professionals. Young professionals are very in tune with their surroundings and can vicariously observe a peer or a manager succeed at a skill or task, and they say, "if they can do it, so can I." While personal mastery significantly influences developing self-efficacy, vicariously observing others and using peer modeling is a very effective source.

No Brainer
Identifying those in your professional and personal ecosystem who are great
at a particular skill you want to develop is essential. It would be best to start
observing them and then model their behaviors.

The third source is social pressure or persuasion to develop self-efficacy for a skill

This occurs when you hear, see, or receive verbal or non-verbal cues from others. These cues might be intentional or unintentional, but they influence your development of a skill. Social persuasion can be a powerful leadership tool to encourage others to develop and build self-efficacy. As a leader, you observe a skill gap in a direct report; you take it upon yourself to privately mention it and offer a potential solution for how they can build the skill.

If the persuasion stops, the person may take no action to learn. If the influence you wield as a leader continues, the employee will likely know and develop the self-efficacy needed for that skill. As a learner, be on the lookout for these cues. Watch how others react to you or when they provide you with constructive feedback. This could help you take action to develop a particular skill and build a higher degree of self-efficacy relating to it.

The last source of influence is the emotional reactions that accompany specific skills, tasks, or activities

If you feel anxious or a great deal of stress about a skill, you are less likely to want to start it, learn it, and thus develop self-efficacy. On the other hand, if you feel optimism or hopefulness that you can learn the skill, you are more likely to start it.

The key to emotional reactions relating to self-efficacy is your ability to understand and interpret them in yourself and others. Emotional reactions are a great temperature check for the level of self-efficacy for yourself or others. For example, if you get nervous leading up to a presentation, you might have low self-efficacy for this skill. Suppose you are a leader and notice emotional or physical signs that a peer is experiencing before a presentation. You can identify low self-efficacy and use coaching skills to set that peer at ease and coach them.

Understanding the four sources of self-efficacy will enable you to apply them in developing new hard and soft skills quickly. Self-efficacy is a leading factor in why my suggested approach to gaining new knowledge is learning, applying, and refining it.

Lesson 29 – How to Build Self-Efficacy

Self-efficacy is a breakthrough skill that can be applied across various applications and situations. Our self-efficacy, or feelings and motivation, influence our ability to start and achieve the desired outcome for a task or skill. The techniques needed to develop it applies to small and extensive applications. How you build self-efficacy for leading a small team meeting are the same techniques you would use to learn how to lead a multi-billion-dollar acquisition.

As a learner, once you develop self-efficacy with these techniques I present to you in this lesson, you can apply them to every new task or skill you will need to learn during your professional and personal life.

Here are the top six techniques to build self-efficacy regardless of the skill or task you are learning:

1. Stay in the growth zone

Studies have shown four personal zones of achievement; the comfort zone, the fear zone, the learning zone, and the growth zone. The comfort and fear zones kill innovation and squash a person's motivation to learn. The learning zone is when a person takes in new knowledge. However, it often goes unapplied. The growth zone is perfect. As its name suggests, it keeps you in a constant state of learning, challenging yourself, and working at the fringes of your ability. Not only do you take in new knowledge, but you continuously apply it and are willing to fail. You show personal fortitude by continuing to work towards mastery. This is how you develop self-efficacy.

Image 27: The Growth Zone

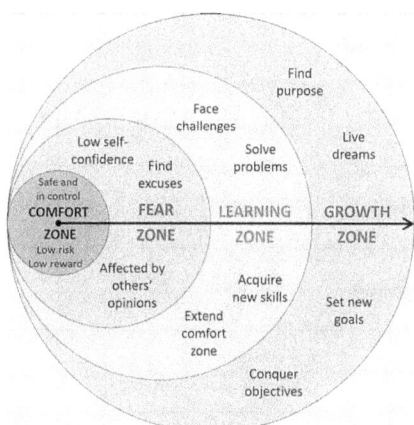

If you stay in the learning zone, you are heading in the right direction but might not develop self-efficacy. To get into and stay in the growth zone, apply these simple tips:

- First, do the things that you like to do
- Next, link courage in trying new things and be willing to face new challenges at work
- Third, make sure to accept that you are going to experience failures. Show that you can learn from them and get feedback as a positive part of learning.
- Last, approach goals slowly and don't over-stress about results on your first pass

2. Set simple SMART goals for your personal development and create a learning roadmap when starting to learn a new task or skill

This tried and tested approach might sound ineffective, but it works. It works when you set goals, monitor them, and strive towards them.

Image 28: SMART Acronym Worksheet Template

S	Specific	• Who is included? • What do I want to achieve? • When do I need to achieve it?	Your responses
M	Measurable	• How will I measure my progress? • How will I know if I my goal is achieved?	
A	Achievable	• Will it be clear when the goal is completed? • Is it reasonable to complete this goal?	
R	Relevant	• Is this goal related to my overall success? • Will it help me advance in my career?	
T	Time-Bound	• How long should it take to accomplish this goal? • When will I check in on my progress?	

Not having SMART personal development goals is foolish. You should have a couple written down and are progressing at all times. They should also be included in your goals at work and shared with your manager.

3. Keep your eye on the bigger picture

A lot of the skills we need to build self-efficacy are root skills such as active listening, how to improve situational awareness, or how to create a meaningful learning goal. But, none of these skills will get you where you want to go. To build self-efficacy, you need to keep your eye on the bigger picture and remember that it will take several skill structures to reach your goals.

4. Remember that bumps, challenges, and failures are part of the learning process

An important technique for developing your self-efficacy skills is to reframe obstacles. Remember, you are operating in the stretch zone, not the comfort zone. The pain and frustration you are feeling are personal growth.

Have you ever had a coach, teacher, or boss tell you, "no pain, no gain?" This is what they were referring to. How you frame obstacles makes the difference between giving up to avoid a short period of pain caused by failing or if you power through the uncomfort and pain to build self-efficacy.

Warning
Don't forget the five ways to fail. Embrace each as a learning experience.

5. Try, try, and try again

You didn't learn how to ride a bike the first time you tried. You didn't learn how to read, solve an equation, or throw a ball well your first time.

It took dedicated practice and a willingness to skin your knees a little before mastering it.

Inconsistency in applying new knowledge and skills is where most of us fall short. If you don't try and continue to try after failure, you aren't going to improve.

6. Find a coach or mentor to support you

This person has to be a trusted advisor. Someone who can give you brutal, candid feedback without the fear of hurting your feelings and damaging your relationship.

This might sound like a bridge too far and something that would take too much effort on your part, or it could be too burdensome for the other party. But it is a valuable way to learn a skill or task and develop self-efficacy.

Proof of this is the billion-dollar executive coaching industry. Senior leaders and executives spend perfect money for someone to mentor them as they learn how to be an executive and develop the skills needed to be successful. Why should you not afford yourself the same level of development in your career?

Before you pay for an executive coach or a professional certification course, seek a trusted leader at your work to be a mentor. This is much more effective!

These six techniques are proven ways to build self-efficacy when learning something new.

Remember the learning cycle. You start with taking in new knowledge by learning; then, you have to apply it and refine it. These techniques then fit nicely into the applying and refining stages.

Learning is not enough; you must apply and refine new knowledge to build self-efficacy.

Lesson 30 - How to Coach Someone Towards Self-Efficacy

Being a people manager has shifted away from the supervisory oversight of making sure direct reports complete tasks towards becoming a coach that teaches, elevates, and enables the proper behaviors of team members to execute on a higher level. Learning how to coach a person towards self-efficacy is a critical root skill often missed during leadership education and on-the-job training. The difference between an employee with self-efficacy and one without it is easy to recognize if the leader is adequately trained and attentive.

An employee with a high degree of self-efficacy will display the following characteristics:

- First, they seek complex tasks to learn and master. These problematic tasks are treated as opportunities, not challenges.
- Next, they set challenging personal goals and commit to completing them.
- The third characteristic is that they increase their efforts at work when they hit snags or face setbacks to their goals.
- Fourth, they don't make excuses for failure. They generally exhibit more self-awareness and associate failures with a lack of knowledge or skills on their part. Not how others have failed them. Concerning recognizing a lack of knowledge, individuals

with high self-efficacy know that new knowledge is acquirable and is proactively sought out.

- Last, they approach unknown situations with the confidence that they can learn as they go while executing. In other words, they display courage.

As with these positive characteristics, some tell-tell unfavorable signs indicate an employee has low efficacy.

- They will shy away from or put off taking on tasks that they don't know how to start or complete.
- Second, employees with low self-efficacy will be slow to create goals and have a wavering commitment to achieving their personal goals.
- Next, they are quick to point out their deficiencies and any obstacles to their success rather than focusing on how to learn and complete a new task successfully.
- Fourth, as a leader, you will notice that they are quick to slack off or give up quickly in demanding challenges.
- Another sign is that they may be slow to recover confidence in the wake of failure, setbacks, or constructive feedback.
- Last, emotional signs of anxiety, stress, and depression might be present.

To learn how to coach employees and peers toward developing self-efficacy, you should focus on these seven leadership actions:

Leader Action 1: Be an effective communicator

Clear, concise, and two-way communication is the first action you can take toward developing one's self-efficacy. You have to provide candid and constructive feedback. Not ridicule that is filled with sarcasm or poorly placed jokes.

Leader Action 2: Use multiple learning mediums

When you identify a skill or task where development is needed, leverage multiple learning mediums and sources; this will improve their learning experience and the possibility of turning learning into new behaviors.

Leader Action 3: Ensure safety

As part of the learning experience, as a leader, you need to create an environment of safety where an employee can try to learn a new skill or task and know that expertise is not immediately expected.

> *Warning*
> *Nothing stops learning faster than in an unsafe environment.*

Leader Action 4: Encourage freedom

Next, allow employees freedom of thought and action in their daily work and personal development. This promotes innovation and helps to create a learning culture.

Leader Action 5: Provide learning opportunities

As you monitor the employee's building self-efficacy, identify opportunities for them to practice the new skills. This will also create an opportunity for you to provide constructive feedback.

Leader Action 6: Provide the right level of support

When it is appropriate, more help and support might be needed. When this is the challenge, assign a mentor to the employee.

> *No Brainer*
> *Pick someone with the expertise to coach the employee on the skill or task they are focusing on.*

Leader Action 7: Lead by example

Last, you must model the behavior and skills you want to see from the employee developing self-efficacy.

> *Warning*
> *If you take the "do as I say, not as I do" approach, then the employee will not fully accept your coaching and not develop the self-efficacy needed to succeed.*

If you are an attentive leader, you will recognize individuals with high or low degrees of efficacy. And by applying these actions, you can coach your direct reports or peers toward developing self-efficacy on any number of skills or tasks.

Knowledge Check
Section 4
Knowledge Check

Grab a pen and paper and answer the questions below to check your new knowledge from Section 4.

1. What four breakthrough skills make up the How You Feel domain?
2. Compassion is _____ from empathy.
3. The most utilized action that shows compassion is _____.
4. Having tough conversations in the workplace requires _____.
5. Courage is a noun defined as our ability to do something we are afraid of. Since courage is an ability, then there are root skills that can be _____, _____, and _____.
6. A root cause of why we struggle to include others and create an inclusive environment is because we forget to treat employees as _____.
7. Self-efficacy is the belief that an individual has about their _____ to learn, perform, and complete a task to achieve a _____ outcome.
8. What are the four sources of self-efficacy?
9. True or False: Decision-making requires you to have and show courage more than any other skill in the CYA.
10. True or False: Diversity and inclusion are the same things.

(1) compassion, inclusion, courage, and self-efficacy (2) action-driven (3) communication (4) courage (5) learned, applied, and refined (6) people (7) capabilities, preferred (8) Your experiences in the mastery of the skill, vicariously seeing others perform the skill, social pressure or persuasion for the skill, emotional reactions to a skill (9) True (10) False, are NOT the same

Section 5 - The How You Act Domain

At the end of this section, you will:

- Have learned about the four breakthrough skills that make up the How You Act domain.
- Complete several applicable lessons that you can start using today to demonstrate each skill and begin to make progress in your personal development.
- Be able to start interacting with peers, managers, and executives in different ways.

Image 29: The How You Act Domain

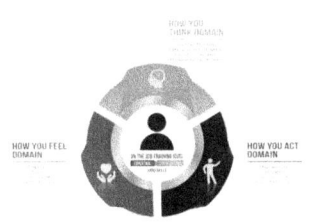

The third domain is the window into a person's soft skills that we use to evaluate and focus most of our efforts on re-skilling. It is how others view and perceive us. Of course, I am referring to How You Act. This last domain is the projection of soft skills through outward-facing behaviors. An outward point through an interaction or other How You Act skill is usually the only way an individual's soft skills can be evaluated and a potential gap identified. Thus, making this domain and its four skills essential for your success.

Quick Facts & Findings of Research Study

- The four breakthrough skills that are part of the How You Act domain are; interactions, adaptability, resourcefulness, and influence.
- More than three-quarters of all soft skills break down during how you act.
- Most skill structures include one or more skills from the How You Act domain.
- Two of the top 5 most sought-after soft skills are part of this domain (Adaptability and Resourcefulness).

Chapter 18
Adaptability

THE SPEED at which you can learn, alter, adapt, and transform the way you work in the wake of organizational changes is a critical skill that often gets overlooked.

In my 2019 benchmark study on soft skills, adaptability was among the top 5 skills that executives valued and looked for when hiring and promoting employees.

My research has concluded that adaptability is part of the How You Act domain in the CYA.

Yes, it has elements of how you think and feels about change, but adaptability isn't a mindset or an emotional influence. It is an action or outwardly projected behavior. Adaptability shows you are altering how you work, performing a task differently, or adapting to a new way of thinking.

To get started, we must distinguish between an individual being adaptable versus the expanding use of change management within organizations.

Tough Talk
You lack adaptability if you struggle with change at work or in your personal life. This critical soft skill is one you should target for improvement.

In recent years, change management has been the preferred response of many organizations' approaches and tries to steer change efforts. While the concept is decades old, it rose to popularity in the mid-1990s due mainly to John Kotter's best-selling book *Leading Change*.

As an organizational discipline, it has a horrific record.

In synthesizing literature sources, we know that many organizations have recessed in their ability to execute change with the rise of change management as a process. Their fault is that they rely on an already flawed process or step approach that typically applies existing techniques for communication and training to address an employee's soft skill gap.

It is my point of view that being good at change, and being able to create an agile organization that can respond to its increasing velocity, requires strengthening employee soft skills—not introducing a change management process, building a change team, or inviting an outside consultancy to manage a flawed approach.

These have been shown not to improve how well an organization changes. Instead, their narrow focus on process improvements to communication and training only realizes small wins.

> *Tough Talk*
> *Seriously! Change management, at its core, is nothing more than employee resistance management that uses the same critically flawed communication, training, and leadership approaches that have been shown to not work in the past. Lipstick… Pig!*

The first benefit of developing the breakthrough adaptability skill is that it is transferable and coachable across all career levels. Once learned and practiced, you will build self-efficacy and be able to respond positively to change throughout your entire career quickly. You will no longer rely on someone telling you why change is needed or how to do it.

The second benefit is that you will quickly stand out among your peers and be able to coach the development of adaptability in others. As more individuals expand their capabilities with this breakthrough skill, your team and organization can respond to new ways of working and performing faster.

This chapter will discuss how you can begin to take quick action and learn as you go to become more adaptable. You will learn how to build personal agility and how being a public learner embodies adaptability.

Lesson 31 – The Secret to Becoming Adaptable

Let's discuss the steps you can take to become adaptable. Adaptability is made up of two distinct components; flexibility and versatility.

Flexibility is your attitude. How willing are you to change?

Versatility comes down to ability. Are you capable of change?

Let's start with versatility

You might recall this from the introduction to this workbook. Knowledge without application is not going to help you reach your goals. This simplified learning approach will maximize your retention and help you achieve your learning goals faster:

- To Learn is to take new knowledge.
- To Apply is to use that knowledge as a new way of thinking or working.
- To Refine is to reflect on the application of your knowledge and make it fit into your situation.

Image 30: The Ideal Learning Approach

You might be wondering why I am revisiting this learning cycle when talking about how to become adaptable. The reason is that this is the first secret to becoming adaptable. If you are confused, that's okay. Let me explain.

You might be scratching your head right now because you, like almost everyone else, have been conditioned to think about change in the workplace as something that others do to you.

Hence, why we started this chapter by discussing the failures of organizations in implementing change management; this is how companies and leaders try to influence you to change and adopt new ways of thinking or working. They don't approach it as an individual soft skill that can be learned, applied, and refined over time.

> *Tough Talk*
> *Remember how I defined adaptability, the speed at which you can learn, alter, adapt, and transform the way you work? The keyword is "you."*

The reasons why organizations don't approach it as a skill is due for several reasons:

- First is the lack of knowledge of how an individual changes psychology.
- Note: My favorite book on individual change is *Tiny Habits* by BJ Fogg, Ph.D. It will change your life!
- Second is the failure to understand the root causes of why teams and organizations fail.
- And lastly, the lack of accountability within their organization to address past failures.

If you are ready to stand out among your peers and reach your true potential, you must stop waiting for others to influence you. Stop waiting for others to communicate the reason why or to train you.

Let's look at each stage in this continuous learning cycle and how they apply to become more adaptable. More importantly, let me show you the decision gates you must go through after each stage.

Learning is taking in new knowledge

While you might associate learning with reading a book, taking a course, attending training, or another grand gesture that requires significant sums of time, learning is a much more straightforward activity that we do all the time. For instance, when was the last time you looked up a topic in a search engine like Google, Bing, or Yahoo? Or listened to an opposing point of view? Or even took a different route to work?

Each of these simple activities was a learning exercise. You took in new knowledge when you searched for a topic. You took in a different opinion by listening to another. And lastly, you learned if a new route was faster or slower than your usual one. Becoming adaptable starts with being open and willing to seek out new knowledge. I refer to this as proactive learning.

Learning

A crucial part of developing adaptability-related self-efficacy is learning how to learn. Yes, that's a thing. Not all of us are great at learning because we were never taught how to learn as working professionals. As such, many of us can improve the way we learn on the job and show improvement in the way we adapt. Let's briefly discuss the differences in knowledge types and how we approach learning.

When we went to school, either our primary education or college, we were primarily taught conceptual knowledge. We were taught about concept theories, classifications, models, and generalizations. We read books, listened to lectures, reviewed our notes, formed study groups, and took exams to show our mastery of the new knowledge. But, while we got educated, we did not develop good learning skills for when we joined the workforce.

On-the-job learning is much more focused on procedural knowledge. This knowledge type focuses on how you perform or take steps to complete a specific task or set, which is different from learning a conceptual theory. This means the way we learn in school no longer applies. We need to relearn how we know on the job quickly.

Here are two tips you can quickly apply to become a more successful adult learner:

1. Be a public learner

It would help if you strived to be quicker than your peers to take action by seeking out knowledge. Another tip for public learning is to create an inclusive learning environment where everyone is welcomed and contributes to the team's overall education and development. Highlight the areas where you have failed and how you learned from those setbacks. Publicly talk about the challenges you face and welcome ideas or recommendations. This illustrates that you have humility and make a significant effort to learn.

2. Make sure to leverage all available resources

Way too many organizations rely only on internal learning and development sources. This means that internal subject matter experts or training documents are the primary source of truth and are the only things available for learners. With so much more information, you need to consider external knowledge or the lessons learned from others. This can help you inject new ways of working and thinking into your organization from external sources in similar situations or have done what you are currently trying to do.

Here are the top ways an individual demonstrates openness and a willingness to seek knowledge:

- Open to Knowledge
- Admits when they are unsure or don't know something
- Willing to listen and consider the view of others
- Can work in the grey (unknown) areas
- Starts a new task fast, knowing that they can learn as they go
- Works through collaboration
- Always happy to teach, coach, or be a mentor.
- Seeking Knowledge
- Asks for help with humility
- It starts with a question.
- Leverages all available resources
- Actively looks for data, opinions, or recommendations from others.
- Quick to experiment with a new idea or concept
- Is reflective
- Looks for or have a mentor they meet with regularly

As you adapt to changes, either personally or organizationally driven, you must show openness and willingness to learn new knowledge for the new ways of thinking and working. Then you must go a step further and seek out knowledge before others try to give it to you.

"What did you do to prepare for today?" asked a brilliant Sales VP in the room just before her team started a full day's worth of training on a new customer relationship management (CRM) system.

This simple, yet impactful question, was met with silence and trepidation from the nearly 50 people looking up at her from their tables. "What is she talking about?" was what one salesperson whispered to another at the table I was sitting at.

After a few awkward moments of silence in the room, the VP smiled and said, "no, I am not asking if you had a good breakfast this morning. I am asking if you took the time to learn about our new system before you came in today." Again, silence.

Her eyes slowly moved across the room, and her head began to nod slightly. "It seems like we have a lot of catching up to do today." She introduced me as the change consultant leading the CRM training for those two days.

You might wonder what that sales VP meant by telling the sales team they needed to catch up since they had not yet been trained. Her point was, why would you wait for someone else to give you knowledge? Any individual on that team in 2005 could have quickly sought out knowledge and demonstrated the first sign of being adaptable. Proactive learning.

As I mentioned, the year was 2005. And that encounter has had a resounding impact on how I learn and teach others to learn.

> *Important Note: I was a change management consultant for several years. Then as I moved up into a partner role, change management was one of the strategy disciplines that my practice specialized in. So, I speak about the horrific record change management has as someone with more than a decade of experience.*

For example, I learned that the first gate you reach and must move through in adaptability is deciding to do something with your new knowledge. You have to make a conscious choice to take action to apply your learnings.

To Apply is to use that knowledge as a new way of thinking or working

Applying is to use knowledge as a new way of thinking or working immediately after learning it. Once you take in new learnings and consciously decide to try them out, you start to apply that knowledge in your real-world environment. This is a crucial step towards developing adaptability. Only through this can you begin to shift your normal, or old, ways of working and thinking to now include your new learnings.

In terms of work-related changes, research has shown that it takes a person up to 66 days to be as sufficient with the change as before. For example, suppose your employer introduces a new software system you rely on to do your regular job. In that case, it will take you and your peers nearly two months before you can perform that work as efficiently as before.

Your goal should be to take quick action and learn as you go when there is an opportunity to try something new at work. This tip is essential. One major flaw common in adult learners is that they hesitate or stall their efforts to learn and apply new learnings for various reasons. One of the leading causes of this hesitation is that many of us wait for others to provide the learning or training. This is not a proactive approach and relies too much on others to teach us. This is how we learned while in school, and it's not ideal for the workplace. To be proactive, take quick action, and know as you go, you should seek out new knowledge without being prompted by a manager or trainer.

> *Warning*
> *Don't wait to start applying changes or new ways of doing things. Waiting is only to your detriment.*

Imagine going into a meeting about a recent process change with your team. Everyone sits quietly, listening to the manager, encouraging them to perform the new ways of working as prescribed. However, you have been proactive in applying the changes, have positive feedback, and can offer the team insights from your early work in adopting them. Once you learn, you immediately use and are further down the learning curve than your peers. How do you think your manager receive this?

So far, you have learned and started to apply your new knowledge. It's now that you have reached a second gate. In this next step, you indeed show that you are adaptable by deciding to refine the change and new knowledge.

To Refine is to reflect on applying your knowledge and make it fit into your situation

Refining is to reflect on applying your knowledge and make it fit into your situation. Here, you link emotional intelligence with adaptability and are reflective of your actions to shift the way you are thinking and working. The goal is to understand how you are doing with the changes and how you can improve your performance.

Refining is an outward projection of mastery; hence, it is part of the how you act domain.

Here are the three most straightforward ways to refine changes and new knowledge to make it your own:

First, find time to pause and reflect on how the changes impact your work performance. How are they impacting your experiences and your attitude towards them? It is here that you can identify ways to make improvements. For instance, let's refer to the example of new process changes from the applying section. What do you do if you find the new process is missing an important step or is taking considerably longer than the old one? During this reflection, you should identify ways to refine it.

Second, find ways to engage others in your refinement efforts. A tip is to form a cohort, or what you might know as a study group of individuals, to learn together. If you reflect on your education, cohorts proved much more effective than working alone to resolve a complex problem.

Last is to set aside time every day to learn something new related to your new ways of working. For example, I set aside 15 to 20 minutes every day on my afternoon calendar to do research, talk to a colleague to share knowledge, or fire up a new application to spend time learning it using dedicated hands-on time. This proactive behavior is how to become a better professional learner and develop efficacy in being more adaptable.

To demonstrate adaptability, you must be willing and capable of progressing through all three steps. This includes making a conscious choice to take quick action and refine your new ways of working.

Lesson 32 - Employing Self-responsibility

I have used the term self-responsibility on several occasions during different lessons. This describes how you, as an individual, are responsible for your thoughts, learnings, actions, and career development.

While other individuals, such as your immediate manager or human resource partner, may play a role in preparing and coaching you, the bulk of the responsibility falls to you. Those who feel it is solely the obligation of others to coach and prepare you for success are just wrong. Having a good trainer or coach is a great way to learn and get ahead, but it is up to you to put yourself in a position to receive and listen to the coaches around you. This is especially true when your organization makes a change. The change could be as simple as introducing new software or a complete overhaul of your job description and daily work activities. No matter what, it is up to you to adapt to the new ways of thinking, working, and performing.

> *Tough Talk*
> *When you lack self-responsibility, you cannot be genuinely adaptable because you are avoiding the accountability of your actions.*

By not having self-responsibility, you can become stuck in self-destructive patterns of behavior that suggest a poor pitiful me or a victim mindset. With this disparaging attitude, your ability to learn and your willingness to try something new rapidly deteriorate. You then start to pull away and alienate yourself from those who can support and coach you through this time.

Recognizing these harmful behaviors is part of the learning process toward self-responsibility to change and adaptability to all circumstances.

To develop self-responsibility, you need to apply three root skills:

Root Skill 1: Self-awareness

By linking this emotional intelligence root skill with adaptability, you become conscious of your thoughts and feelings towards a prospective action or change. This is critical. To have self-responsibility, you have to have self-awareness. You need to know yourself and recognize negativity or avoidance patterns related to learning and performing something new.

You can respond with the appropriate actions that move you forward by being aware.

Root Skill 2: Forming positive habits

We all have poor habits that influence our ability to take self-responsibility. These habits could be how we work, the people we interact with the most, or how we outwardly project our attitudes. As it applies to self-responsibility, positive habits elevate our ability to be more adaptable.

Remember I mentioned the book *Tiny Habits* by BJ Fogg earlier? This is just one area where that book helped me.

For example, if you are always sitting with the same group of co-workers at lunch and you begin to notice their negative attitude affects how you feel, it might be a great idea to stop having lunch with them. Negativity spreads like wildfire. Form habits that are positive and take ownership of them.

Root Skill 3: Accept setbacks as opportunities for growth ad self-development

This element of the entrepreneurial mindset links with adaptability because failing safely and learning from it is good. Self-responsibility is working in the growth zone of your capabilities with the knowledge that imperfection is okay.

The critical action that should come from imperfection is the commitment to learning. If you have shown the courage to try something and change how you work in support of an organizational initiative, it is perfectly acceptable to have setbacks and skin your knees a little.

The second, the third, the fourth time you try the new behavior or change, you will be better each time. It takes self-responsibility to fail and to get back up and try again.

Chapter 19
Influence

IT HAS NEVER BEEN MORE important to yield influence at work.

How you influence others, advance your ideas, and affect how work is performed is a crucial soft skill that most individuals overlook. When I speak about influence as a soft skill, I refer to an individual's ability to get others to act on their ideas, solutions, and encouragement. While it has never been more critical, it has never been more difficult to yield.

Many of us might confuse having influence at work with positionality or having a title with a certain level of authority over others as part of an organizational chart. Having positionality over a person has managerial duties or direct influence over a person or team. This influence means that your subordinates listen to you and perform as you want them to for most work-related tasks.

As you might have already put together, yielding direct influence over a person or a team is not a skill, but you can certainly display many soft skills as a direct leader. While positionality certainly contributes to a person's influence, it is not the only form of influence a person can have in the workplace. Titles or your location on the org chart is not proof that you mastered the skill of influencing your peers and leaders.

Warning
3 out of 4 people believe influence is a byproduct of having authority or

responsibility as a people manager. It is not. This type of influence is known as positionality and not a soft skill. However, everyone, regardless of title, can learn to influence others.

Indirect influence means that you can affect a person, or a team, to follow your ideas, listen to your contribution to thoughts and solutions, and encourage co-workers as a peer leader for them to perform in a manner you desire without having authority over them.

This is a breakthrough skill that takes time to master. Research shows that individuals who strongly influence others have learned how to link multiple breakthrough skills from the CYA to create valuable professional relationships. The most critical breakthrough skills to influence are emotional intelligence, compassion, courage, and interactions. Each plays a vital role in your ability to persuade, be assertive, have just in time impact, convey your ideas and consider those of others.

During this chapter, I define the difference between negative and positive influences. As well as discuss strategies on how you can learn to create workplace influence and expand it.

Lesson 33 - How to Gain Influence at Work

Let's take a few minutes to discuss how you can start to gain influence and the two critical elements that can improve your odds of success with this breakthrough skill.

Here is a bit of brutal truth! Influence in the workplace is a highly sought-after power. Those who have it love it and want to keep it. Those who don't have it are envious and seek to gain it.

The harmful elements of influence are the traditional methods of gaining and keeping. You might be part of an organization where office politics are rampant. It's normal for peers and leaders to backstab one another or jockey for a position, using rumors and conjecture to negatively affect perceived rivals' reputations and successful work. This toxicity is apparent in for-profit organizations at the senior manager or executive levels. The challenge is that it can often pour over to lower-level managers and employees to become rooted in the culture.

These traditional negative approaches in which influence is gained and kept can have lasting effects on an organization's ability to innovate, retain top talent, and stay competitive in the market. These are not good characteristics for an employer to tolerate or an employee to exhibit. I want to recognize that being political and thriving in office politics is a skill. Just not one I would recommend.

The good news is that many organizations are starting to steer away from office politics to create influence by recognizing and learning how to create a more positive, inclusive, and welcoming work environment and culture. In this lesson, I will present strategies to help you avoid office politics and develop the soft skills needed to gain influence constructively.

It is no coincidence that trust is among the most practical and meaningful ways to build influence at work. Both the obtainment of trust and that of influence have to be earned. Your peers or your leaders do not give it freely. It is important to distinguish between the three different types of trust in the workplace and be able to build and maintain each type. Let's quickly look at each.

Competence

The first is trust in your competence. When you trust a person's competence, you know that person has the knowledge, the ability, and the motivation to get the job done. That's the person who can make things happen. If you want to move items forward and get things done, you trust that this person will do it.

Benevolence

The next trust type is benevolence. This is trust in that a person has good intentions toward you. They will look out for you and provide information to protect you or advance your goals. You know that when you're not in the room, this person will not undermine you. Simply put, you know that this person will have your back.

Integrity

The last type of trust is integrity. This type of trust is all about a person's moral character. You know this person always operates with integrity no matter who is involved and how they feel. They will always work according to their principles.

To build trust, you should focus on these three root skills every day:

Root Skill 1: Your superpower

It would help if you were consistent and predictable in your actions, emotions, and performance. This is a trust multiplier. People who are consistent and predictable quickly earn our trust.

Root Skill 2: Be open to feedback

Listen and accept constructive feedback. No one trusts a know-it-all. We want to trust individuals who are open to ideas and active listeners and welcome feedback so they can make personal improvements.

Root Skill 3: Become valuable

Establish yourself as a subject matter expert or a quick learner. Never speak out of place on a topic you know nothing about, or interject an uninformed opinion. Focus on what you know and stay away from issues you don't. A helpful hint is not to be afraid to say I don't know, but I will find out.

Along with trust, you can gain influence through positive interactions in the workplace. You will need to link these breakthrough skills from the CYA to build trust and gain influence. Other breakthrough skills are equally important.

For instance, as you demonstrate emotional intelligence, courage, and critical thinking, your peers and leaders will open up to you and expand your influence. Like trust, you must show meaningful interactions over time before gaining meaningful influence.

The best ways to do this are to show courage when others don't and lean towards optimism.

Courage at work is speaking up or taking action when others do not

You are willing to speak to right a perceived wrong or offer a recommendation first to get a stalled conversation moving. Having courage at work is admired by those who lack it, and they will naturally start to rely on you to say what they are thinking or speak for the team. This provides you with influence.

Years ago, I was called into a room with six fellow directors while at a company offsite. Our manager, a Sr. VP, had been accused of sexual harassment. The CEO, the CHRO (Chief Human Resource Officer), and a company lawyer were in the room. It was pretty clear to the seven of us coming into the room that this was very serious.

As the CHRO outlined the complaint, we all sat astonished and listening intently. At the end of his speech, he asked if we had noticed any unwarranted advances or inappropriate behavior. Crickets...

After a LONG minute of silence, I spoke up.

Lean towards optimism to create positive interactions

Please note that I don't say you need to be an optimist. Being a constant optimist is not for everyone, but it is a trait people love and want to follow. When you want to gain influence, it helps if you are optimistic about the situation, the team, or the organization.

As you might have experienced in the past, it's effortless to follow a pessimist. But, if you think back to your experiences with a negatively slanted person, after a brief period given to them complaining about work, a person, or a project, this pessimist doesn't yield influence for long. However, a person who leans towards optimism while recognizing the realities of the situation will gain influence.

If it is your goal to gain influence at work, you need to build trust with your peers and organizational leaders. Determine the three types of trust you can use to establish it yourself. Next, make sure you link the break-through skills of interactions and courage. Lean towards optimism and show courage when others do not.

No Brainer
With increased trust, it is easier to demonstrate courage in the workplace.
Start with building trust in your relationships.

Lesson 34 - How to Expand Influence at Work

As you gain influence, it would be expected that you would want to expand it.

As you follow the strategies to gain influence at work, you will notice that teammates and your organizational leaders are turning to you more. They seek your counsel, asking you to take on new, higher-profile tasks and projects. But above all, you are building trust with them and positioning yourself for success and advancement.

The most crucial tactic you can take in the near term is to remain stead-fast in performing at a high level, building trust, and not overextending yourself. As your influence solidifies with your current environment, your appetite for more will increase. Naturally, you will want to extend your influence and take on more prominent roles and responsibilities.

When you consider expanding your influence in the workplace, timing is critical. It would help if you made sure that you have demonstrated your ability to impact your current network positively and performed well on the higher-profile tasks you have received. If you have doubts about either, it is not the time to expand your influence. But, if you have been a strong contributor for some time, have made a difference on your team, and have performed well, then it's time to look at the next steps.

Here are the top six ways to move out of your current comfort zone and increase your influence at work:

1. Network

The first way to expand your influence is a no-brainer; you will need to network. More people in higher positions in your organizational chart need to know your name to expand your influence. It is that simple. As your reputation grows, start to identify leaders or peers in other parts of your organization that you can bring into your network. Remember the lessons taught in the lesson on networking and apply them in your efforts to expand your influence.

2. Be amazing in your current job

To build a great professional reputation and to get your name known by senior leaders in your organization, you need to be exceptional in your current job. Very few get noticed or advance in their careers by being average performers. If you want a great reputation and influence, you need to be an above-average performer and stand out among your peers.

> *Tough Talk*
> *Every one of us thinks or believes we are exceptional at our job! But, if no one else thinks you are, then YOU ARE NOT! If you are getting poor performance reports, constantly being given constructive feedback, or being told that more is expected, you have room for improvement.*

3. Continue to develop your expertise

Another way to build your reputation, and expand your influence, is to make sure to continue to develop expertise. Higher knowledge and performance can lead to expanded influence. As you prove subject matter expertise in your current role, start to look for new ways to learn and expand your knowledge. The best areas to focus on are learning the tasks or activities your boss currently does. Or those in a place where you would want to advance your career. Use learning to position yourself as an invaluable member of the organization.

4. Grow the diversity of thought in your work area

The fourth way to expand your influence at work is to grow the diversity of thought in your circle of influence. Be the constant voice in the room, asking others to empathize when decisions are made or including others in the decision-making process. Make sure to include others in your decisions as a leader. If your organization doesn't use design thinking techniques to develop personas, journey maps, or ideates, then make sure you are a leading voice to introduce and expand its use.

5. Link your critical thinking skills

The next way to expand your influence is to link your critical thinking skills with your influence. Be a critical thinker and always try to plan two to three steps ahead. Have the answer or the recommendations ready before you get asked for it. Be proactive in identifying, ideating, and solving issues and challenges facing your team and organization. Be bold and have self-efficacy in your critical thinking skills.

6. Don't mix or waste words

The last way to expand your influence at work is not to mix or waste words. Be direct when speaking with senior managers or executives. Be compassionate when teammates need a soft voice and an ear to listen. Be personal and treat peers and employees like people capable of feeling and thinking for themselves.

Apply these six tips to expand your influence. But remember, the key to gaining and expanding influence is to be the complete you. Influencing those at work requires considerable breakthrough skills. Learn them, apply them, and develop self-efficacy for each of them.

Lesson 35 - How to Power Through Negative Influencers

As we explore influence at work, I need to address how to identify and navigate individuals who wield negative power over the peers or the leaders you wish to influence positively. These individuals are excessively pessimistic and make a great effort to project their attitude and way of thinking onto others. In almost all cases, the negative Nancy or the pessimist in the group is a very influential voice on a team. It is not because they are the loudest. It is primarily because of their ability to leverage social tools, such as gossip, and unfavorable perceptions, to assert pressure on those who oppose their point of view.

Allowing negative influence to grow includes decreased trust among all team members, drastic loss of productivity, stunts innovation, and causes a breakdown in formal communications because the informal channels are more potent at forming opinions.

No Brainer
Spotting those who yield negative influence in your place of work is pretty straightforward. It is what you do from there that makes a difference.

Here are seven signs that a person is negative and could potentially affect others through their influence:

1. First, they frequently say, "that's not my job," when asked to take on a task or do something above and beyond their regular duties.
2. Next, they think they have already paid their dues and are quick to point out.
3. They feel seniority is the most important factor when assigned work or a leadership role needs to be filled.
4. Another sign is that they lead the meeting after the meeting. This occurs after a leader hosts a meeting; they are the informal peer leader who gathers everyone to discuss what happened in the meeting. This is a very detrimental behavior.
5. Regarding peer-to-peer relationships, gossip is always the word of the day. This person is known as a source of how gossip spreads.
6. Have you ever heard the phrase "misery loves company?" Well, that is this person. A negative influencer in the workplace will apply peer pressure to keep people at their level and within their sphere of influence.
7. The last sign is that they quickly take the credit and blame others for shortcomings.

There are a significant number of reasons why individuals become negative influences. These reasons could include an uncomplicated pessimistic attitude or learned helplessness after repeated rejection or being passed over multiple times for promotions. However, the most common reason that causes individuals to become negative influences is due to lack of leadership. Mainly, two aspects of leadership are at fault.

First, their team leader failed to keep them engaged effectively. This could be due to a lack of inclusion, a lack of compassion on the part of the leader, or the lack of positive interactions between the two individuals. The leader's responsibility was to have the awareness and soft skills needed to identify a negative attitude and take steps to improve the situation.

The next reason a leader has failed this negative influencer is that they have allowed the poor behavior to continue and fester among the team. That shows that the leader could lack the courage to take action to improve or remove the negative influence from the team.

> *Tough Talk*
> *Failure of leadership is not an excuse for negative behavior to build, fester, and take over the culture.*

If you are experiencing negativity and wish to navigate these individuals safely, you need to follow a few tips:

Tip 1: Stop Participating in it

To start with, do not participate in negative activities or conversations. Stay above gossip rumors and away from the meeting after the meeting. Yes, for a while, you might be the subject of gossip or the topic of discussion after the meeting because you are not part of the negative in-crowd. Accept this reality, but don't let it get out of control. If you are harassed, follow your organization's policies in reporting it.

Tip 2: Be the positive example

The following way to combat negative influences is to show courage and speak up to protest their behavior. Call them out on specific comments and hold them accountable for their behavior. Your peers will respect you more, and your courage might positively affect your leader to take action.

The courage to speak up isn't an invitation to start a conflict. Show emotional intelligence when confronting negativity.

Tip 3: Escalate it (when needed)

Which is the third tip, involve others in support of rooting out and squashing negative influencers. You are not alone in your feelings. You are not alone in this stand against negativity. Use your network to find allies that will support you in taking action to stop the negativity. It will take courage, but the potential rewards of eliminating any negative influence will significantly outweigh the risks.

As you gain and expand your influence, you will eventually run into individuals who show the signs discussed in this lesson as negative or pessimistic. You do not need to allow this behavior to affect you, the work you are performing, or the relationships you are building. Apply any of the three tips to eliminate your team's negative Nancy and power through negativity.

Chapter 20
Interactions

For better or worse, how we interact with peers, managers, and executives at work plays a significant role in how we are perceived and evaluated.

As proof, have you ever heard"you never get a second chance to make a first impression?" This phrase suggests that first impressions, or your first interaction with a person, are crucial in forming a positive and lasting connection.

While first impressions are important, how we interact with others goes well beyond first interactions. Learning to manage your interactions is a crucial part of the CYA, linking how you think and feel domains with outward projections. As I have previously stated, the entire premise of the CYA is your ability to develop a set of breakthrough skills, link them, and take action to stand out among peers to do amazing things. Interactions are the main stage for your performance.

As part of your learning with the CYA, you have focused on improving your critical thinking and entrepreneurial skills. To demonstrate them, you identify an opportunity at work that no one else has noticed. You select the data you need, analyze it, and now have a couple of recommendations for your boss.

But, at this exact moment, the only skill that matters is your ability to present your findings and recommendations effectively. This interaction dictates whether you can demonstrate your new skills and whether your recommendations are accepted or rejected. As with this example, you can see how your ability to interact with others successfully will substantially impact your career development and how others perceive you.

Here are a few examples of the outcomes of everyday workplace interactions :

- If you have an outburst in a meeting, you are perceived to have low emotional intelligence.
- If you are always late with turning in routine tasks, you are perceived as poor at executing.
- You are perceived as having little or no influence if you always give excuses for why others aren't following your directions.

I can go on and on about how different everyday interactions influence your reputation and career projection. Instead, I want to point out a word I have used several times in this introduction that is vital for you to grasp and comprehend. That word is perceived.

A former colleague of mine in the Human Resources space once brilliantly stated, "perception is reality's co-pilot."

In other words, the reality might be that you have emotional intelligence and your outburst during a meeting was a simple mistake. However, the perception of others weighs heavily on how you are perceived and your professional reputation. It is your responsibility to influence that perception in a favorable way to improve or to take action to change how others perceive you.

Now, you might be thinking, this all sounds a little like office politics and that I am suggesting that you have to be aware of how your interactions are perceived, and you need to be calculated with your actions. Well, maybe that is part of the message. But, more importantly, you need to learn how to interact positively to build self-efficacy and become second nature. This will take refinement.

Tough Talk
Your self-awareness in recognizing the importance of interactions is the first step in improving them. How do you solve a problem? By realizing you have one!

During this chapter, I will explore some basic tips on how and when to create meaningful interactions at work. As well as present some pointers on making the most of anxiety-causing interactions, such as interviewing and giving presentations.

Lesson 36 - How to Master Everyday Interactions

Interacting with your team and peers every day is an important way for you to build your credibility, demonstrate your skills, and build your professional capital. Whether you are the team leader or a direct contributor, this is true, working hard and trying to do your best. This lesson focuses on the everyday, routine interactions or what would be considered our usual ways of working.

These interactions are fundamental to our success, and there are four ways to improve these everyday interactions and show others that you are engaged in your daily work.

The best way to improve everyday interactions is to be present

This means that you are present in the moment. If you are having a discussion, a one-on-one meeting, or a quick chat at the water cooler, stay off your phone or computer. Show the individual or set of individuals you are speaking with that there is nothing more important at that moment than them. You are present by keeping eye contact, staying engaged in the conversation, and avoiding picking up your phone to check your texts or emails. You are focused on the person or persons in front of you. Not a device.

Warning
Looking at your phone is often a habitual reflex. But doing it during a conversation sends the wrong message to the person you are speaking with. An excellent way to avoid this reflexive habit is to put your phone away so you

can't reach for it.

Remember, communication goes both ways, and non-verbal cues are just as important as verbal ones. Another tip is to focus twice as much energy on listening as you do talking. I am sure everyone has heard why we have two ears and just one mouth. Then why is it so hard for us to listen to what others are saying, understand them, and show compassion?

Warning
The number one failure in the office is a lack of communication.

Better communication in the workplace is done by improving four elements: frequency, medium, inclusion, and visuals.

1. Frequency

Increase the frequency of messages. It takes the average person 5 to 7 times to hear something to take action or to comprehend it fully.

2. Medium

Get away from emails. Face-to-face talks, phone calls, and handwritten notes are alternative mediums that will yield much better clarity and follow-through when action is needed. If more than half of your office communication is done via email, you are doing things wrong.

3. Visuals

Use more visuals. Research has shown that we respond better to visuals than written or spoken words.

4. Inclusion

Expand your circle. We all have a group of people that we consider part of our inner circle. These are trusted advisors and the individuals we use as sounding boards when we need to vent. This is perfect. But what about putting more people in your second layer? Those you speak with often, those you can ask advice from, and whom you would be receptive to their ideas or suggestions.

No Brainer
Expand this second level in your circle and build more relationships through networking.

As you improve these four elements, you must show equality and equity in your actions. Give voices to everyone by asking their opinion, asking them for a recommendation, or helping them be included in critical tasks and decisions.

This increases the diversity of thought and action. It improves engagement, performance, innovation, culture, and many other factors you should consider. Be the person on the team that includes everyone. Be the person who allows others to contribute and to learn. Be the person who breaks the silos that create the bureaucracy everyone complains about but does nothing to improve.

No Brainer
Of the four ways to improve daily interactions, showing equality and equity in your actions is the most powerful.

With improved communications, you will create more positive interactions. Positive interactions are good for morale, building teamwork, and humanizing each other in the workspace. They are great opportunities to expand your relationships and break down barriers in communication.

Positive interactions could be great offsite, team-building exercises. Or they can be design thinking workshops, group, or team learnings, joint presentations, and seminars with other parts of the organization to eliminate silos. The key is identifying ways to bring more people together to do great work versus allowing them to operate alone.

By learning and applying these techniques to improve your daily interactions, you will see more favorable outcomes, and better communication will become the norm and stand out among your peers. Remember, it will take time to apply each of these, and don't expect to solve decades of over-communicating via email in just a couple of weeks. Focus on changing your behavior, and everyone else will follow.

Warning
Notice that I did not recommend humor as a way to improve everyday interactions. Most people try to use humor with little effect at work. I would suggest not attempting it.

Lesson 37 - Leading by Example

Gandhi was credited with saying, "be the change you want to see in the world."

These words are a powerful message about leading by example. Most people confuse being a leader with having the responsibility of people management. When in reality, they are not always the same. Another point of clarification is that having a title doesn't make you a leader either. Nor does not having a title prevent you from being one.

There are a ton of different definitions for what makes a good leader or what actions they should take to lead by example. I scoured the research and drew from my own experiences in consulting, leadership coaching, and as an executive to create a set of three leading practices that everyone, no matter their position, can do to lead by example.

Tough Talk
Every person can improve multiple aspects of how they approach leadership. No one is the perfect leader.

Leading Practice 1 - Be authentic

Find a balance between being personal and being professional. Give yourself and others permission to laugh, smile, and genuinely enjoy being part of the team. The second part of authenticity is showing your shortcomings and publicly committing to improving them. Model continuous learning and be open that you don't have all the answers.

Warning
No one likes a know-it. By showing vulnerability, you demonstrate your will-ingness to take calculated risks, fail and learn. This is leading by example.

Leading Practice 2 - Have a strong presence

Be bold when you act, speak, and recommend potential courses of action. Having a solid presence means that you talk when others are silent. But this doesn't mean that you don't listen. It means you have an informed point of view and dare to take a stance in projecting your thoughts. Having an informed point of view indicates that you have considered and listened to all angles and differing opinions.

Part of having a solid presence is to be decisive and purposeful in your work. You are a master at executing tasks, volunteering for leadership opportunities, and being willing to take the initiative when others are not up for the occasion. You outperform your peers with everyday assign-ments and model accountability by taking responsibility for your and your team's work. The buck stops with you.

Leading Practice 3 - Be Adaptable

Hiring managers, executives, human resource partners, and peers love the individuals they can count on to be adaptable to change and move at the velocity of ongoing transformation. By being adaptable, you are quick to take action, willing to learn as you go, and are not afraid of failure. You show personal agility in rapidly responding to new requirements, processes, and ways of working. You take self-responsibility in learning and being a peer mentor, whether it's a formal or informal role.

When working with your peers to adapt to change, you give them the freedom to act and use their talents. You encourage them to follow your lead in acting and fail fast as long as they learn from their experiences.

Next, you give your peers the mentoring, the coaching, and the time they need to be successful. You recognize that their success equates to the team and the organization's success. It is a personal mission for you to be part of the solution, not part of the resistance to change.

No Brainer
Being a leader doesn't require a title. It doesn't require having direct reports
under your name in the organizational chart. It requires you to be authentic,
have a strong presence, and learn how to lead by staying ahead of the so-
called change curve. Exhibit these traits, and you will stand out among your
peers, do amazing things, and become a better leader.

Lesson 38 - Rising Above Passive Aggressive Behaviors

Passive-aggressive behavior is pretty typical in workplaces. Passive-aggressive behavior is defined as indirect resistance and avoidance of confrontation.

You might see an employee pouting. Yes, like a small child. You might see an increase in procrastination, individuals avoiding each other, or an increase in finger-pointing.

These behaviors are detrimental to the efficiency and productivity of individuals and teams. They are also harmful to the creation of long-term professional relationships. Would you want to trust and have to work with someone petty enough to pout when they don't get their way at work?

To prevent this negative behavior from starting or stop it once it starts, you must confront it head-on. I will examine steps you can take either as a person being affected by someone else's passive-aggressive behaviors or the steps you can take as a leader who is witnessing the behavior play out in front of you.

Let's start by looking at an individual affected by having another person using passive aggression against them. This is a tough spot because you might not often know why the behavior is being directed toward you. It could have been something you said, did, or didn't do. It could have been something the other person heard, or it could be simple workplace jealousy.

The initial step is to privately meet with the person, stating that you have noticed the behavior, and ask them what has caused it. This discussion will go one of two ways; they will either calmly deny it or have an emotional outburst. Most often, they will deny it. Be ready with specific examples that point to passive-aggressive behaviors if they do.

The best technique is to say, "I have noticed these behaviors {insert example}, from you, and I thought they were a bit passive-aggressive. My apologies if I am wrong, but I don't expect to see them or experience them again now that I have cleared the air."

The next step is crucial; you must document the conversation with a note. What you said, what was said in return, and how you asked for the negative behavior to stop. A couple of simple ways to make a note is to email yourself or put it in Google Doc or OneNote file that is saved to the Cloud under a personal folder.

Returning to the above example, if the behavior does not stop, elevate it to your boss, citing the note you made for yourself. This is why managers have jobs. It's okay not to agree with peers and not to get along with everyone in your office, but no one should aggressively make things difficult for you. If this person shows this negative behavior towards you, rest assured that they are directing it towards others. Be the difference in the office and elevate it.

As a leader, you should never apply passive-aggressive behavior. It erodes a team's culture as quickly as your direct reports of confidence in your ability to lead. You should also not stand for it when you notice it happening on your team.

Usually, passive-aggressive behavior is caused by misunderstandings between two or more individuals. Instead of trying to solve the misunderstanding, they flee from it and resort to shallow behavior.

No Brainer
Part of your job as a leader is to create a team culture free of passive-aggressive behaviors.

The first step is to call it out in private with each individual if you see this. Tell them that you have noticed a change in their behavior and want to know what has changed. Ensure you get both sides of the story before offering an opinion or a recommendation.

Please encourage them to solve it for themselves. If, after a few days, you don't see a change in the positive, then intervene. Pull them into a meeting together and ask, "what has been done?" since you spoke to them individually.

Then listen. Remind them that you expect them to resolve their disagreement and move forward. This again puts the pressure and the ownership of the resolution on them.

> *No Brainer*
> *The best way to correct negative behavior is to have the person exhibiting the behavior develop a solution to improve it.*

If they can not resolve it, then set forth a plan of action that changes the dynamic between the individuals. Make sure your actions match the situation and address the behavior of the person acting passively-aggressively. Not the person who is on the receiving end.

To end passive-aggressive behavior, you have to confront it head-on. You must have a zero-tolerance stance towards it if you are a team leader. As an individual, you need to have the courage to elevate it if your actions to resolve it have failed. It is crucial to your well-being at work and your success.

Chapter 21
Resourcefulness

So much of our ability to execute and get things done at work depends on our resourcefulness. Resourcefulness in the workplace is finding ways to overcome obstacles or difficulties quickly.

This breakthrough skill is part of the how your act domain and links to multiple other skills in the CYA.

My 2019 research study showed that an employee's ability to be resourceful was a top 5 soft skill managers and executives valued and looked for when hiring and promoting employees. Furthermore, three-quarters of the survey participants selected resourcefulness as a critical skill for career advancement.

This is why resourcefulness is so essential. Many of us work in complex, multi-layered organizations that historically operate as a collection of departments and silos.

For several years, I worked at one of the world's largest companies, measured by the number of employees. It had nearly 400,000 global team members. Their size and scale created so many silos that learning how to navigate them and get things done was a critical skill to demonstrate and master for those employees interested in advancement. Employees of this tech giant even had a phrase to describe the inner workings; they called it the "blue goop."

For those of us who are part of a large company, our ability to solve persistent problems or execute often requires us to break silos and navigate layers of bureaucracy to influence individuals who don't usually work with us to get things done.

And then, a few of us might be part of smaller organizations or start-ups where we wear multiple hats, which means that we are responsible for continuously learning how to be more productive, which requires us to be more resourceful in our actions. In smaller companies, each team member has to be resourceful in finding solutions and getting things done with more limited resources.

So, whether you are working at the world's largest organization or at a small, rapidly growing business, your ability to find ways to overcome obstacles or difficulties quickly will be essential to your success and career advancement.

Lesson 39 - Organizational Navigation Requires More Than a Map

Navigating the culture and informal processes of working within an organization is essential for career advancement and outperforming peers.

Every organization, department, and team has a culture and bureaucracy that uses unspoken processes to advance or stall work and accelerate or prevent change. Identifying these informal processes and the individuals who control them or know how to navigate them is vital in navigating your organization successfully. You need to understand how things work and which relationships are most important to getting work done.

Let's start with which items influence how things get done and how they are prioritized. Knowing these four influencers will help you in navigating your organization:

1. What are your organizational goals? Down to team and individual goals.
2. How decisions are made. Don't be fooled into thinking this is a documented and formal process.

3. What are the critical work cycles and financial reporting deadlines? You can be sure these influence how things get done, resourced, approved, and prioritized in an organization.
4. How are resources allocated to perform work? Who selects employees to perform tasks? Who or what department holds the purse strings? All of these influences matter when learning how to navigate your organization.

Once you know and comprehend these four influencers, you can start to navigate the formal and informal processes. However, I am sure you have heard that it's who, not what, you know. Figuring out the motives, intentions, and how to leverage the different personalities in your organization will aid you in being able to navigate getting work done and avoiding pitfalls.

Let's take a quick look at a few different personas most employees fall into and how they are motivated. Note that a person can be motivated by more than one factor and straddle more than one persona.

The Purist

This person is driven by the details and relies on formal documented processes to get work done and make decisions. These are usually your partners in Human Resources or Finance. Signs that an individual is a Purist is that when you ask them for help, they point you towards a Wiki site, a SharePoint, or a document that needs to be filled out to process your request.

Purists are good allies know when moving information around or finding information. Since they are stickers for details and processes, they can slow things down and become bottlenecks. When working on a task or a project, make sure to loop these team members in early so that you know all the details and expectations that need to be completed.

The Navigator (my favorite)

As you might have guessed, this individual knows how to navigate the formal and informal organizational processes and has the know-how who makes decisions. They are motivated by getting the job done. These are important allies, and you should focus your networking efforts on forming as many mutually beneficial relationships with Navigators as possible.

> *Warning*
> *These individuals are usually easily identifiable, meaning everyone knows who they are. Since everyone knows who they are, they might be stretched thin and pulled in several different directions by many co-workers. Make sure to build a mutually beneficial relationship so that you are helping them out too.*

The Historian

These individuals are motivated by organizational norms and rules. Unlike the Purists, they are not processed-driven, nor are they stickers for the details. They like standard operating procedures and structured decision-making. They want things to stay the same and quickly point this out by saying, "that won't work here" or "that's not how we do it."

Historians are usually organizational veterans and have been with the company for many years. While these individuals are great at giving you historical insights, they offer little value in getting work done and might not be worthwhile in forming relationships with.

The Players

These individuals are motivated by what's best for them. They are quick to jump on or lead popular initiatives. Even quicker to run when things get tough or go sideways. Personal reputations are very important to these individuals, who are conscious of taking risks. Their primary motivator is trying to get ahead, and they have been shown to tend to undermine others who are outperforming them.

> *Warning*
> *Players are usually very easy to identify. These are not individuals; you want them as allies. Be cordial, but keep them at a distance.*

Remember to know the four items that influence how work gets done and the four personality types individuals can be themed by. Once you know these, you can start to navigate your organization better.

Grab pen and paper and start a list of how your peers, co-workers, and leaders fall into these four persona types.

Table 4: Typical Organizational Personas and Motivations

Persona Name	Motivation
Purist	Motivated by the details and relies on formal documented processes
Navigator	Motivated by getting the job done
Historian	Motivated by organizational norms and rules
Player	Motivated by what's best for them

Next, ask yourself if you have the right relationships with your co-workers. If not, how can you improve it? Lesson 41 is an excellent place to start.

Lesson 40 - Breaking Silos & Barriers

In the 1990s, a buzzword emerged to describe the desired effect of breaking down silos within the organizational structure. That word was synergy.

Leaders across all organization types used this word to define how they wanted teams, groups, departments, and subsidiaries to interact and cooperate more so that their combined result was greater than the sum of their efforts.

For decades, the pyramid leadership shape with departmentalized teams has dominated how organizations were structured and outlined how each employee, team, and department fit within that layered enterprise. While reading an organizational chart was super easy, this structure limited interaction between individuals, teams, and departments. Hence, silos were created.

When silos are present in an organization, work is performed by defined parameters, decision-making, and the location influences the org chart. Collaboration between the silos is difficult to establish and maintain.

Extensive research has concluded that silos strain organizational effectiveness, undermine innovation, and pit employees and managers against each other for resources. Government is an excellent example of a siloed organization.

> *Warning*
> *Silos strain organizational effectiveness, undermine innovation, and pits employees and managers against each other for resources.*

For more than 30 years, most organizations have been trying to eliminate the adverse effects of silos. Despite this effort, they are still an anchor present in many organizations. You might currently be or have worked at a siloed company in the past.

As we examine how to break silos, I should be candid with you. This is challenging work. It takes strategic direction, individual buy-in, and relentless execution to break and maintain a dynamic organization that is not defined by boundaries. Let's first briefly talk about the best strategic actions that can be taken and then how you, as an employee, can better break down silos.

If you are a senior manager, or an executive, looking to build synergy and create a more dynamic organization, these are the five best approaches to take:

1. Unify the organizational vision and goals

Every individual needs to understand and align with the vision and have individual performance goals tied to achieving organizational objectives.

2. Expand collaboration and knowledge sharing using technology

The market is filled with cost-effective tools and mediums to help break silos by quickly expanding collaboration and internal knowledge sharing across individuals and teams. If you already have these tools and don't believe you are maximizing them, spend some time evaluating and understanding their use.

> *Tough Talk*
> *It is not uncommon for an organization to have good tools in place, but employee buy-in, or utilization, might be low. Does your organization already have the right tools, and are they not used well?*

3. Optimize your organizational structure by creating a cross-functional or a shared team structure

In the age of agile, design thinking, and employee experience, there is no reason why teams, and projects, especially those in the IT department, should work in a silo. The next time a project kicks off, look at the team and ask yourself if it is diverse enough.

> *Tough Talk*
> *Organizational and team structure is usually the reason why silos have been created. But, the people aspect prevents you from knocking them down.*

4. Develop Leaders

Many undesirable behaviors that create silos come from senior managers and executives jockeying for positions. This is due to individual ambitions and the lack of knowledge of how other teams or departments' daily activities and capabilities contribute to the organization. Set up job rotations for high-potential individuals and senior leaders to build a more unified mindset.

> *Tough Talk*
> *Every organization can do a better job at developing its current and next generation of leaders. Don't fall into the trap of thinking that your leaders are good.*

5. Set up an innovation hub within your organization

It should be separate from day-to-day operations, fully funded, and allowed to create its own culture and direction. Lockheed Martin began its Skunk Works more than 75 years ago. IBM has its Garage, and many other organizations have dedicated cross-functional and funded teams focusing on innovation for internal and external products and processes.

Now, let's shift gears to review the actions you as an individual can take to create collaboration and expand your knowledge and influence in the organization while breaking silos. Here are the top four suggestions:

1. Expand your network

The best way to knock down barriers to collaboration and eliminate any silos hindering your work is to expand your network simply. Networking is a crucial root skill that significantly contributes to your resourcefulness at work.

2. Think Win-Win

Take a page or a chapter out of Stephen Covey's famed book, *The Seven Habits of Highly Effective People*. Think, win-win. Too many times, individuals try to collaborate on a problem or opportunity that benefits them. What's in it for the other individual or team if there is no benefit? And worse, it just adds more work that needs to be done. Think win-win, and give others a practical reason to jump in feet first with you.

3. Win over the right influencers

If you are thinking win-win and are expanding your network, make sure to aim high in the organizational chart. Don't just focus your efforts on a peer-to-peer network. Identify the right influencer on the other team or department, and go after them to present the opportunity to collaborate or form a cross-functional team.

4. Expand the diversity of thought

Incorporate design thinking techniques in your efforts to improve collaboration and inclusion. Make meetings and workshops more productive and inclusive by using the activities and methods to get everyone up, moving, and thinking outside the box with improved ideation and solutions.

Regardless of your position within an organization, if you suffer because of silos and the barriers they create to improving collaboration and efficiency, then take action to break them. Be bold in your activities, recommendations, and execution. Form new relationships by linking your other breakthrough skills.

The mere fact that you have identified the silos in your organization and you are taking a calculated risk by working towards breaking them, you will rise above and stand out among your peers.

> *No Brainer*
> *Design thinking is a great way to break norms. But it's not the only approach. Do your research to find what works best for your team and organization.*

Lesson 41 - Learning how to Network

> "Networking is the #1 unwritten rule of business success."
>
> Sallie Krawcheck, CEO of Ellevest

I agree with Sallie.

Networking is a little bit of an art and a lot of skill. When employed successfully, you can use it to form new professional relationships that create or expand opportunities, share information, or help enlist others to support your efforts. Networking involves the social interactions required to meet, engage, and quickly create a meaningful dialogue with a stranger.

Suppose you have seen a peer or leader who is excellent at networking. In that case, they seamlessly work in a room, moving from interaction to interaction, collecting business cards, exchanging phone numbers, and creating reasons for a follow-up activity. It can look like an art form. But, it's just a soft skill. Some have mastered it and developed self-efficacy. At the same time, others of us are still looking for the right level of courage.

What I mean by we are still looking for courage relates to the findings of multiple studies in the last twenty years. Several of them have shown that more than 75% of us don't actively work to create or expand our professional networks. The leading cause isn't a lack of time or the lack of understanding of its importance. It is fear.

Specifically fear of being rejected and not knowing how to do it successfully.

Let's be honest; networking is a little like dating and approaching a person for the first time. Some of us do or did it well; others have to wait for our moment. The good news is that, like other skills, you can learn how to network and develop self-efficacy for it. This lesson outlines three simple rules and several techniques for how you can become a master networker. You can apply these rules at conferences, trade shows, and even within the office.

Let's start with a common misconception.

Good networking is not about the size but rather the quality of your connections. If you attend a conference and meet 100 new people, but none are in a position or willing to help you with an opportunity or information, those 100 new connections aren't very good. But, let's say you are at the same conference and make three new connections that you quickly find have a similar career or work interest and challenges. There is now a reason to have a follow-up conversation with these three new connections. One that is mutually beneficial.

Rule 1: Focus on creating mutually beneficial connections.

By now, you have heard me say this multiple times. There is a method to my madness. Remember, networking is a two-way connection. If you are networking, then it is safe to assume so is the other person. You are both trying to figure out if there is something that the other person can help you with or add value to. So, the first rule is to focus on creating a mutually beneficial connection. To do this, apply these four easy tips:

1. Find the right venue. Make sure the venue or event you are networking at aligns with what you like about your work or adds value to you. Don't waste your time if it doesn't.
2. Ask simple questions and listen. You are networking, not solving complex problems. Save that for the follow-up activity with your new connection.
3. Don't sell. Don't sell a product or a service or oversell yourself. People hate being sold too. Stay away from this behavior.
4. When speaking and asking questions, make it more about the other person than yourself. Follow the Bobby Bowden rule. 99% of the conversation is about the other person, and only 1% of it is about you.

Rule 2: Have a purpose

Like all other activities, those we do with purpose are more likely to succeed.

The first tip is to have a purpose by setting a goal for your networking efforts. What are you looking for, and what would benefit you the most from this networking event?

Next, know what you offer the other person. Remember, you are both networking and looking for a mutually beneficial connection. Being able to help the other person is important to make a good connection.

The last tip for having a purpose is to find a reason to follow up or politely move on. Remember, networking is about the quality of connections. If there is no mutually beneficial rapport, then politely move on.

Rule 3: Be human

Meeting new people can be both a little intimidating and fun at the same time. Enjoy the experience and show that you are human.

Smile. People will not approach someone who looks miserable or looks too serious. So, have a welcoming demeanor.

> *No Brainer*
> *A pleasant smile goes a long way in getting people to speak to you.*

It's ok to show a little humor. Don't be full of jokes and keep things professional, but people like to smile to laugh and love it when their jokes are laughed at. Adding humor to networking can break the ice and keep a conversation moving.

Rule 4: Be a part of the conversation, not the center of it

People love to talk about themselves. Which naturally means that we love to talk about ourselves, too. Take advantage of other people's natural tendencies and focus the conversation on them. What are their interests, needs, and issues at work, and how can you help them?

Networking at an event or office requires the same activities, and you should follow these tips. To get started, you will need to link another breakthrough skill from the CYA; courage. As you start to network more, you will get better at it. This will make you more resourceful and get things done faster and better.

Put yourself out there and go for it!

Lesson 42 - Finding a Well-Placed Mentor

One of the best ways to learn how to navigate an organization, perform at a higher level, and expand your career prospects is by finding a well-placed mentor. Mentors are wise, passionate volunteers willing to support the personal development of other employees, and they can be a massive ally in developing your career. What I mean by being well-placed is a person who is at least one level higher than you in the organization and is considered a strong leader among their peers.

Here are a few benefits of finding a good mentor:

- Studies show that individuals with a mentor have higher job satisfaction.
- You will have an experienced person to bounce ideas off and receive advice from
- Individuals with mentors tend to have more developed emotional intelligence, and they execute at higher levels.
- You can get access to more data and create more trust.
- Having a well-placed mentor also gives you greater visibility among other organizational leaders.
- You will also gain an ally who supports you when it comes time for advancement.

When wanting to get a mentor, you should first check to see if your organization has a formal mentoring program. I love formal mentoring programs but realize that most companies today don't have them. The best person to check with is your Human Resource partner. In the event your organization does have a formal program. Make sure to express your interest and ask how you can be included in it. Make sure you have a couple of good reasons for wanting a mentor ready if you get asked.

If your organization does not have a formal mentoring program, be proactive in obtaining one. You should take a few steps to get a well-placed mentor, but first, let's talk about the qualities you should look for in a good mentor.

The first trait you are looking for is good rapport

This might sound funny, but there needs to be a connection, mutual respect, and admiration. This personal connection is vital to support the bond between you both.

The next trait is for your mentor to know the organization well

Both the formal and informal processes. They need to help you learn and perform at a higher level and be able to introduce you to others to expand your network.

They should be well-respected and have a good reputation in the organization

You don't want to tie yourself to someone negative, who might not be aligned with the organization's culture or may be on their way out.

> *No Brainer*
> *As you search for a mentor, make sure they are willing to give you at least an hour of their time every two weeks. Or at minimum, one hour a month. You should look for more in a mentor than a name alone. You need a coach and an organizational navigator. Choose someone who sees your potential and the value of developing the organization's talent.*

The last trait is a mentor with a career progression similar to the one you want to take or has a skill set you want to mature

For example, if you want to spend your career in marketing, you shouldn't go after a mentor who is in logistics. Find a commonality between what you want in a mentor and what they can offer.

Now that you know what to look for, here is the best way you should approach the identified person and ask them to be your mentor.

If you know the traits you are looking for in a mentor but don't know anyone who is a good match; you can ask for help to identify one. Your immediate manager, or your HR partner, will be able to help you. You might have already identified someone with the traits you are looking for. If so, how you approach that individual will be critical.

If you have an existing professional relationship or are acquainted with them, approach them directly one-on-one. Schedule 15 minutes with them or ask them for a few minutes after a regularly scheduled meeting.

Once you are with them, follow these quick, easy steps in making your pitch in asking them to be your mentor.

> *Warning*
> *If you are too scared to ask someone to be your mentor, they are probably not the right person for you.*

This first part is crucial. You must ensure your potential mentor knows you want to discuss career development and personal growth. During these opening moments, share your desired three to five-year career plan and why you are passionate about this career path. You might get asked about a long-term goal, have one ready but don't lead with it.

If you are an early professional, don't tell your potential mentor that you want to be CEO in the next 20 years. Focus on the near term and goals that you want to accomplish.

Next, demonstrate emotional intelligence and self-awareness by high-lighting known personal shortcomings or skill gaps. This step helps to emphasize that you are serious about personal growth and will work hard to make improvements. It also shows that you have given this great thought, have an action plan, and know what you need help with.

Clearly state how that person would be a tremendous help as your mentor. You have outlined a three to five-year career plan and a couple of personal development gaps; now is the moment to ask them to be your mentor. Be straight, don't beat around the bush or sidestep your request.

Make sure to mention what type of support or time commitment you expect. Your expectations are crucial information for them to know.

Now sit quietly and wait for them to respond. Suppose they say yes, set up a first meeting with them within the next few business days. Act fast while they are interested. The first meeting is a get-to-know other better discussion and an opportunity for discovery. So, I recommend a 30-minute meeting over coffee. Get out of the office or away from the desk for this first interaction. This will help set everyone at ease and allow the conversation to flow more manageable.

If they say no, be ready for how they might reject your offer. You should ask your immediate supervisor if they say they are not the right person. Politely tell them that you considered that. But, you believe they would be a better match for the skills you are looking to develop. If you don't have a great relationship with your immediate supervisor or are new, gently point that out.

Suppose your potential mentor says that they don't have the time. Simply state that you would be willing to change your time commitment expectations. But remember not to reduce the time by too much and stay at least one hour each month at a minimum. Stay firm here, and don't let time commitment scare them off.

This is just an initial excuse in the hopes you will take it. If you are sure that this person is whom you want as a mentor, stay strong and insist that you can be flexible. If they push back again, there might be an underlying reason, and their commitment to your development might not be necessary. Ask them if they could suggest someone who would be a good mentor for you.

Having a mentor is always a wise idea as you grow in your career. It would help if a trusted advisor would listen to you, give harsh feedback, and keep your best interest in mind. If you don't currently have a well-placed mentor, I advise you to find one and start self-improvement.

Use the traits outlined during this lesson to identify the best person for you, and then use these tips to approach that person. Be bold, be courageous.

Knowledge Check
Section 5
Knowledge Check

Grab a pen and paper and answer the questions below to check your new knowledge from Section 5.

1. What are the four breakthrough skills of the How You Act domain?
2. More than _____ of all soft skills break down during the How You Act domain.
3. Adaptability is made up of two distinct components:
4. _____ in your attitude. How willing are you to change?
5. _____ comes down to ability. Are you capable of change?
6. When you lack _____, you cannot be genuinely adaptable because you are avoiding the accountability of your actions.
7. Three-quarters of the survey participants selected _____ as being a critically important skill for career advancement.
8. To prevent passive-aggressive behavior from starting or to stop it once it has started, you need to _____.
9. What are the four personas most employees fall into regarding how they are motivated and act?
10. The best way to knock down barriers to collaboration and eliminate any silos hindering your work is to expand your _____.

11. True or False: Studies show that individuals with a mentor have higher job satisfaction.
12. True or False: Interacting with your team every day is essential for you to build your credibility, demonstrate your skills, and build your professional capital.

(1) interactions, adaptability, resourcefulness, and influence (2) ¾ (3) Flexibility and versatility (4) self-responsibility (5) resourcefulness (6) confront it head-on (7) Purist, Navigator, Historian, and Player (8) Network (9) True (10) True

Chapter 22
Creating Your Personal Architecture

AT FIRST GLANCE, I would understand if you have a lot of apprehension about creating your architecture. Trust me; it is a shared reaction.

You might not appreciate it at this very moment, but there is irony in your apprehension about getting started. In Chapter 17, you were introduced to Self-efficacy, one of the twelve breakthrough skills that are part of the CYA. The exercise of creating your architecture is a perfect way to apply and refine that soft skill.

> Note: Self-efficacy is individuals' belief about their capabilities to learn, perform, and complete a task to achieve a preferred outcome. Simply put, self-efficacy is a driving force behind your motivation to start creating your architecture.

If you missed it, the irony is that you need to strengthen one of the twelve breakthrough skills in the CYA to alleviate your apprehension about starting this exercise.

Before I show you the steps you will need to take in creating your first draft, let me call attention to a few areas where most individuals struggle.

The Slope of the Vertical Line Matters

Ideally, your architecture should form a right triangle (~90 degrees) as it rises from primary structures to aspirational. The broader base created by your primary structures is those with which you do well or have developed self-efficacy. These are learned, mature, and perhaps mastered skill structures that form your foundation.

As you step up from primary, you move from learned structures to those you are actively learning. The indented design of the architecture should help you prioritize your learning by putting additional structures into the top three layers. This promotes staying in the growth zone (developing & emerging) while also allowing you to envision the future (aspirational). This is one of the ways that you can maximize your retention and successfully apply the 12 breakthrough skills that make up the CYA.

Depending on the career stage (or if you change jobs), you might have a narrow foundation and a thicker middle or top in your architecture. If this happens, you are attempting to learn too much at one time. Starting at the top, you should eliminate structures to form a shape until it resembles a right triangle. Image #31 shows the architecture of a recent college graduate who joined my team. Image #31 highlights the four different slope angles I often see.

Image 31: Illustrates the four different slopes for an architectural plan and their meaning

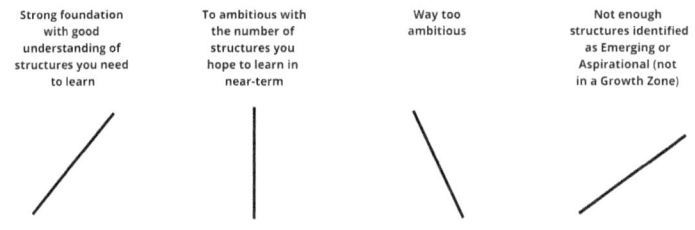

Don't Suffer from Size Envy

Your architecture is just that, your architecture.

We have different experiences, education, traits, values, and aspirations. When creating their architecture, individuals' biggest mistake is not correctly self-assessing their skill structures. There are two primary reasons for this:

1. An overdeveloped sense of self-worth in thinking we are better than we are is the leading cause.
2. At some psychological level, we are all consumed by size! We think bigger is better (except for diamonds and sports cars), so we instinctively try to create a more extensive architecture. To do this, we become very liberal in how we self-evaluate ourselves.

To prevent size envy, I suggest your initial architecture be a snapshot of your current state. This should help focus on the skill structures you apply today (Primary) and those you are learning. This encourages you to hone in on the skills you are using today and those critical to your near-term success (i.e., those that are performance magnifying).

> *Warning*
> *Yes, I keep a complete (historical) architecture that outlines all the skill structures that make up my Complete You. This is primarily for self-reflection. I encourage everyone to create a full version. Just not the first one you make.*

The most significant determining factor in a person's architecture size is their experience level. It would make sense that a senior executive with 30 years of experience has more primary structures than an early professional with less than five years on the job.

One of the most honest self-assessments I have observed came in 2021 from a young professional hired just out of college. At his 90-day review, he was asked to create his first set of skill structures and personal architecture. His honest assessment of his current skills and learning opportunities was brilliant. It clearly showed his strengths as a Business Analyst straight out of college and where he wanted to develop further. Image #32 was one of his skill structures, and image #33 is his architecture.

> Note: Working for Skill Dweeb, all employees are required to create their architecture for their 90-day review. These artifacts are then used as part of our employee development plans. This process will be outlined in my upcoming book on coaching using the CYA.

Image 32: Being Proactive skill structure and skill card for this early professional

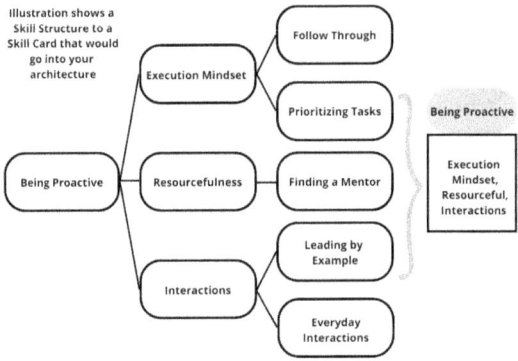

Image 33: The above structure is displayed as a card in the Primary Structure in the early professional architecture

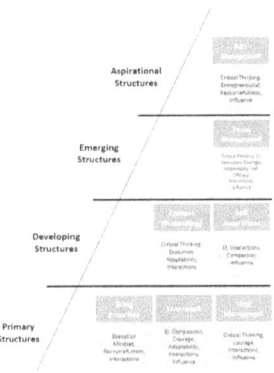

Tough Talk

Please don't lose sight of why you create your skill structures and put them into your architecture. This personal development exercise lets you analyze your soft skills and those you need to learn to rise above and stand out among your peers. The number of primary structures you list only matters if you can apply and refine them to meet your current situation.

Don't Get Stuck on the Steps

"The code is more what you'd call 'guidelines' than actual rules."

-Hector Barbossa, Pirates of Caribbean Curse of the Black Pearl

Your skill architecture will consist of many different and connecting parts that don't occur naturally and must be created with thoughtful consideration and effort. The process you will take isn't set in stone or a series of mandatory steps you must follow. Instead, consider the best practices and tips recommended here from seeing hundreds of individuals create their architecture.

Here are the two reasons why you should approach the following steps as guidelines and with the knowledge that they might need to be modified:

1. I (or anyone) can't understand your current and future skill needs.
2. Self-responsibility is a root skill taught with Adaptability (Lesson 32). You will need to take ownership of your development and be willing to take time for self-reflection (another root skill found in Chapter 10, Emotional Intelligence).

Creating your architecture shouldn't be a quick exercise where you follow a set of predetermined steps that result in a document. Instead, it should be a thought-provoking, unbiased assessment of the soft skills and structures you have developed thus far and, more importantly, those that should be obtained through learning, applying, and refining the CYA.

Keeping the twelve breakthrough skills in mind will be vital as you progress through these steps. To help you do that, here they are again:

Image 34: The Complete You Architecture™

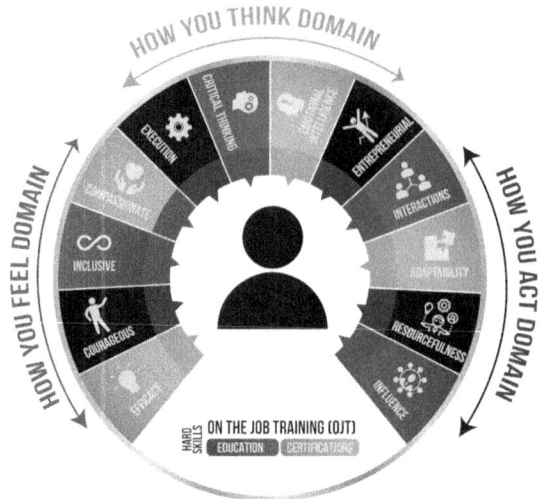

Why work hard when you can work smart

I am a techie. Not in the sense that I understand the nuances of cloud computing, artificial intelligence, or even how crypto-currencies work. No, I am a techie because I use technology to make my life easier in all aspects of my life.

For example, I used Scrivener, a popular application for writers, to organize and simplify my writing process to complete this book.

My family and I use an electric spin mop to clean our tile floors at home because we can do it in half the time, and it gets the floor just as clean as any other mopping option. Our friends made fun of us until they saw us do it. Now they all own one!

This is why we start this discussion on creating your architecture with technology. If you recall, I mentioned in Chapter 8 that I use SmartArt in Microsoft PowerPoint to build and maintain my skill structures. For my architecture, I also use Microsoft PowerPoint. This allows me to quickly develop and keep everything in a single flexible location. Then save it soon to a Cloud account.

Everyone has their go-to application or work preference. I have seen structures and architectures created in spreadsheets, word processors, and even pencil and paper. Choose a method that is best for you and get started. You will learn as you go. Below are three simple steps you can follow to create your first architecture.

> *No Brainer*
> *My first rough draft was using pencil and paper. I could quickly brain-dump information into a notebook, and once I was satisfied with everything, I put it all into PowerPoint. It has lived there ever since.*

Step 1: Create a professional vision statement

A professional vision statement places your career ambitions and passion into an inspiring sentence that describes the direction you wish to head.

Starting here does two critically essential things at the same time. First, it jumpstarts the self-reflection process by having you think about what you want out of your career. Think of this not in terms of a title or a certain salary level but how you want to be remembered. What will be your legacy?

Second, you have begun to identify your Aspirational skill structures. After you write out your professional vision statement, ask yourself what structure your future self will need. One or two of these structures are at the top of your architecture.

Examples of good professional vision statements from past client workshops:

- I will become a well-known and respected influencer in the food industry, revitalizing how food is produced and marketed to make healthier products to help people live better lives.
- I will become a leader in my organization, helping transform it into one that respects all its stakeholders.

- To become the kind of teacher that changes students' lives for the better, educating them about the history, the joys, and the meaning of life.

Here is how to create a professional vision statement:

1. Start by envisioning yourself five to 10 years in the future. What could you be doing that would make you the happiest?
2. Make sure it's relevant. At thirty, if you were to have asked me what I wanted to do in my career, I would have told you that I still wanted to be an astronaut. That was in no way possible and thus irrelevant.
3. Add in purpose. Each of the examples above has a meaningful sense that isn't tied to extrinsic goals.

So, what skill structures will you need if you want to be an influencer in the food industry? If you're going to change students' lives for the better, how do you first improve yourself?

Write down these first skills structure and add it to your architecture as Aspirational.

Step 2: Build the middle

The CYA intends to help you learn the twelve breakthrough skills that are most important to your career. This means that the structures that make up the two middle layers in your architecture are the most important to you to rise above and stand out among your peers.

> *Tough Talk*
> *Don't be fooled into thinking that your primary layer structures are more important. If you already had the right skills to achieve your desired success, you would not have completed this workbook.*

There are two ways you could approach building the middle layers.

The first is my favorite. It requires you to link your emotional intelligence root skill of self-reflection with courage. You need to ask yourself: What is holding you back?

As you consider this question, start writing down your thoughts to ensure you capture each in as much detail as possible. This list should be why you suspect you have not achieved prosperity in your career. Or at least not to the degree that you thought you would have been able to accomplish by now.

Before completing this workbook, when asked this question, most individuals would unconsciously point to external influences such as timing, not being given enough opportunity, or even past managers being bad. But not you. You have started to learn a set of soft skills that will allow you to reflect on your career and be able to analyze it through a new lens critically.

I often observe this when individuals who have completed the CYA start to think about it.

They start to pinpoint specific activities, relationships, and opportunities that have been missed or were not taken full advantage of. With your new knowledge, it becomes more natural for us to think about specific interactions or experiences that negatively affect our ability to advance. Here are a few of the common mishaps that I often hear about:

- I missed an opportunity to take the initiative, and a co-worker grabbed it instead, and are now reaping the benefits of improved trust with your manager.
- I struggled through a client or executive presentation, which hindered short-term prospects.
- You lost your cool in a team meeting and made a couple of comments that you now regret

These are all simple activities and opportunities which impact your relationships, reputation, and career advancement. As you make your list, start to analyze these shortcomings through the skill structures you struggled to apply or those you didn't attempt because you didn't know how to.

Warning
Be careful not to be over-prejudicial and demeaning towards yourself. Try to think objectively about the twelve skills you have just learned and how you could now apply them.

This brainstorming exercise will result in a set of structures and corresponding soft skills that will need to be added to your Developing and Emerging Layers.

Using external sources is the second way to identify potential skill structures to add to these two middle layers. The two most popular sources are:

1. Your direct manager, coach, or mentor
2. Your quarterly and annual performance reports for the last few years (or any other formal or informal review documents)

The first way of asking for constructive feedback from a manager is a double-edged sword. Yes, the primary job of a people manager is to coach and develop their teams to be successful. But that doesn't always translate to people managers having the necessary soft skills to know how to coach and give someone good feedback. These challenges managers have were discussed in Chapter 14.

Tough Talk
If I were to think about my 20-year career, I have had about 12 to 14 managers. Only about a third of them would have been a good source of constructive feedback if I were to ask them, "what soft skills do I need to focus on to improve my performance?"

The good news and the better side of the sword are that some exceptional managers have a passion for people development and the know-how to coach their direct reports successfully. So, there is no harm in asking your manager or coach, "what soft skills do I need to focus on to improve my performance?"

Warning
You might be saying that your boss hasn't been very supportive of you in the

past. There could be many reasons why you might feel that way or why they were not supportive at the time. But don't let that detour you from asking.

The best advice you could get is to schedule a specific time with your manager in a 1:1 setting. If you are in an office environment, schedule thirty minutes with them using your calendaring function in the email. The subject line put "Discussion on Career Growth and Skill Development."

Then in the body, put a brief description of the topics you want to cover and why.

Image 35: Sample email to a manager

Your performance reviews are the second external source to help you identify potential skill structures. These can often offer you golden nuggets of helpful information. Sometimes, the specific area you can improve is directly called out. Most often, you will need to read between the lines.

Below are a few feedback examples from some of my past performance reviews. When you look at these comments, ask yourself which of the 12 breakthrough skills could have helped me make improvements.

1. "I would like to see you take more risks and speak out more during team meetings."

This is a No Brainer. The manager told me exactly what they wanted to see from me. This screams several different skills found in the CYA: Courage, Emotional Intelligence, Critical Thinking, Interactions, and Influence. Can you think of any others?

2. "For this year, I want to see you spend more time helping the team improve our client offerings."

Here is where you need to read between the lines a little. What was this manager asking me to do? She was asking me to collaborate with the team more, so I could contribute to innovation. Any time you see "spend more time," that directly pulls on time management and prioritization (Execution Mindset). The word "team" suggests an opportunity for Interactions and Influence. The last part of this comment mentioned: "improve our client offerings." This is a firm nudge by my manager to be more innovative. Which skills in the CYA relate to being more creative?

3. " You achieved your overall sales goals but missed one of your target product goals."

The valuable information is a little more hidden in this last comment. It is a classic example of a manager giving you constructive feedback hidden behind a compliment. What stands out in this comment from an annual performance review I received in 2006?

I did an excellent job in one area but not in another.

For a bit of context, I was 123% of my total annual sales goal and hit two of the three target product goals. However, my manager then used this line to give me a "Meets Expectations" versus "Exceeded Expectations" on my review, which tied directly into my merit increase for that year. So, it cost me money.

Despite me still being bitter over it, what skills could have been applied to this comment?

Maybe critical thinking, resourcefulness, entrepreneurial, and execution mindsets will ensure I hit that third product goal. And perhaps a little emotional intelligence, courage, and interactions so I could professionally confront my manager on the unjustified rating.

To identify Developing and Emerging structures, look towards yourself first and then pull in external sources to aid you in creating these layers.

Warning
Don't forget to prioritize the performance magnifying skills that will help you most right now for these two layers. It is standard for us to be self-degrading and eager simultaneously by having too many different structures to improve on through these exercises.

Step 3: Know Your Strengths

We all have known soft skill strengths. These are a combination of natural talents and learned characteristics that we have built a high degree of self-efficacy.

The most effective way to build your Primary Structure is to start in the present and work backward in your career. To do this, ask yourself:

1. What skills and structures do I show mastery over every day?

2. Next, what do I have to offer on a regular cadence (weekly or monthly)?

You will start to pull together a set of the most relevant structures to your current work.

No Brainer

If you get stuck trying to think of structures, then list out the twelve skills of the CYA and start to put checkmarks next to the ones you exhibit mastery over each day. The week and month. This can help you turn those skills into links and structures.

As you work your way back from daily, weekly, to monthly, you could potentially get to structures you haven't exhibited in over a year. This is where you stop. The reason is that it's a dormant structure if you have not used it in over a year.

A dormant structure isn't lost knowledge. This means you don't know if this structure and the skills that make it up would be included in your Primary structure today because you don't apply it. Since you don't know, it should not be included in your current state architecture.

No Brainer

As you identify your known skill strengths to place in your Primary Structures, you will undoubtedly start to reminisce on the significant moments in your career when you could masterfully exhibit these skill structures. This is a combination of social and experiential learning that you will need to master the CYA.

Image 36: The Ideal Learning Approach

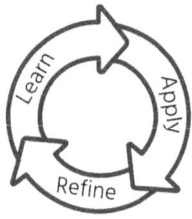

Once you list the structures and skills that you apply regularly, all you have to do now is place them in your architecture as Primary. Remember, this can be done in a variety of ways. You can use a notebook or put your architecture into an application like I started to do with PowerPoint. The choice is entirely yours.

Image 37: Architecture Template

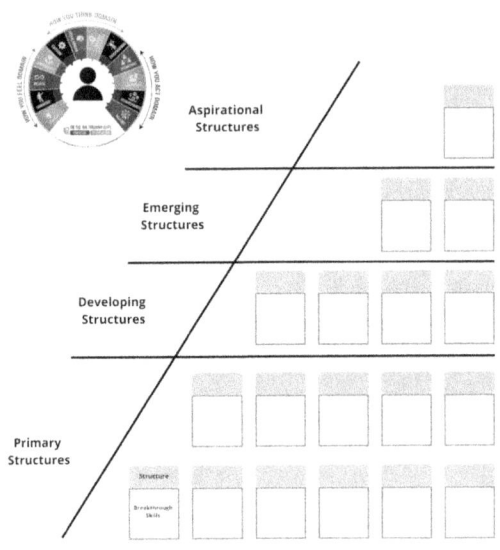

Throughout this chapter, I have outlined several ways in which you can start to build your personal architecture. As you progress through the process and reflect on your skills, you will demonstrate high self-efficacy and courage. You are already linking some of the skills outlined in this workbook and getting closer to standing out and rising above your peers.

This is your Complete You Architecture™.

Afterword

You. And you alone are responsible for your personal & career development. The Complete You Architecture™ provides a research-driven framework to create your skill architecture by learning, applying and refining the twelve most important skills for your long-term career success. Now you must decide which of the three domains and which of the breakthrough skills should be part of your architecture.

By completing the 40+ lessons in this workbook, you have learned valuable tips, tricks, and ways to start demonstrating elevated soft skills immediately. Now, you have reached the first gate of showing that you are adaptable. Do you decide to apply your learnings?

If so, get ready to rise above and stand out!

Thank you for the purchase of this workbook. I am confident that if you apply and refine the skills outlined in the Complete You Architecture™, you will achieve new heights in your career. I wish you all the best!

- Dr. Chris Bradshaw

www.ingramcontent.com/pod-product-compliance
Lightning Source LLC
Chambersburg PA
CBHW060906120626
46553CB00001B/219